ALL SAI

Culture

Current Titles

Concepts in the Social Sciences

Culture

Reinventing the Social Sciences

Mark J. Smith

Open University Press
Buckingham · Philadelphia

2573970

Open University Press
Celtic Court
22 Ballmoor
Buckingham
MK18 1XW

306
SMI

email: enquiries@openup.co.uk
world wide web: www.openup.co.uk

and
325 Chestnut Street
Philadelphia, PA 19106, USA

First Published 2000

A catalogue record of this book is available from the British Library

ISBN 0 335 20319 1 (hb)   0 335 20318 3 (pb)

Library of Congress Cataloging-in-Publication Data
Smith, Mark J., 1962–
    Culture : reinventing the social sciences / Mark Smith.
      p. cm. — (Concepts in the social sciences)
    Includes bibliographical references and index.
    ISBN 0-335-20319-1 — ISBN 0-335-20318-3 (pbk.)
    1. Culture   I. Title.   II. Series.
HM621.S55   2000
306—dc21   00-037364

Typeset by Type Study, Scarborough
Printed in Great Britain by St Edmundsbury Press, Bury St Edmunds

For Harold and George

Contents

Prologue: Culture and the Postdisciplinary Imperative

This book started life as a response to a perplexing question which I heard at a discussion group: 'Why is culture now such a challenging concept in the social sciences?' It seemed so obvious that culture was tremendously important to any kind of discussion about social inquiry that I was initially taken aback by the need to raise this question. Surely, the whole of sociology and anthropology, a great deal of politics, geography, social policy, social scientific methodology, some of economics as well as a sizeable part of history have all been concerned with culture. As the discussion unfolded, I realized that the participants talking about the importance of a 'cultural turn' saw the recognition of culture as fundamentally new, as if no one had spotted its existence before, while those willing to argue against tried to focus on political and economic factors as the final court of appeal for explaining the social. The response from the cultural turners was to criticize the problems of essentialism and foundationalism in attempting to ground the social in the material organization of society. I went away from this discussion somewhat troubled by the way the argument had developed and how the two camps of culturalists and materialists had emerged.

All the participants were right to highlight the things they saw as important yet in their 'battle-mode' none had addressed what culture actually meant. More than that, I began to think about how it was the 'meaning' of the 'cultural' that was at stake (not whether culture itself was important or not). The supporters of the cultural turn had stressed something very important – that the social sciences should take culture seriously – but actually what they had missed was that social scientists already had taken it seriously. Much of the history of the social sciences concerns approaches which had culture and its consequences at the top of the agenda. For instance, the study of civility and citizenship had long been a key interest of political studies while geographers had been exploring cultural issues ever since they became interested in people as well as rocks and water. Some social sciences, like economics, however, are just better at hiding their cultural leanings behind a facade of 'instrumentality' and 'rationality'. Psychologists have only recently realized that 'the mind' has always been a cultural space and that this had been obscured by the scientific search for some underlying truth or set of causal mechanisms which could explain social behaviour. In all these cases, cultural meanings are tacitly involved in the process of knowledge construction.

There had not been just a turn to culture. Something much more significant had happened – culture was being understood in very different ways. It struck me that some further investigation was needed, not on the recent emergence of 'culture' but in order to provide some kind of map about how culture had been and is seen in the social sciences. This meant that we had to acknowledge that approaches to culture had variety. It was not so much a cultural turn as a cultural swivel. Straight away, I realized that one discipline alone could not provide the range of tools to answer this question. Even a discipline like sociology, for all its cultural leanings, remained isolated from many of the cultural questions raised in studies of the state, the economy, the mind, space and place and so on. Interdisciplinary research, while good at posing new questions and highlighting parallels in different fields of knowledge, still suffered from the disciplinary affliction – the belief that the answers to these questions could only be solved by the rigorous work conducted within strict disciplinary domains, with each discipline offering a different slice of the explanatory cake. As a result, thinking about culture does offer something new – a new opportunity to break out of the disciplinary mode of thinking to forge a postdisciplinary approach which tramples across boundaries and synthesizes good ideas and useful research strategies whatever their location. This became the start of a postdisciplinary project to explore what culture has meant and what it could mean in the social sciences. I have argued at length elsewhere for the adoption of a postdisciplinary strategy when addressing the issues of knowledge construction (Smith 1998b) but here we have an opportunity not only to develop this project further but also to begin to flesh out what a postdisciplinary analysis of a substantive object of analysis could mean in the reinvention of the social sciences. Before embarking on this narrative, one proviso comes to mind. I hope to offer a wide ranging account of the significance of culture in this short book but I will not be able to produce an exhaustive account of all approaches to cultural relations and processes. Inevitably, some studies which form part of the growing corpus of cultural studies will be left out and some cultural theorists will not be dealt with in an exhaustive way. The somewhat limited role of this intervention, then, is to draw out parallels between shifts in the study of culture and social scientific practices.

A Genealogy of Culture: from Canonicity to Classification

Culture is an important but can be a slippery, even a chaotic, concept. It can mean a great deal when its scope and relevance are clearly defined and yet also very little, especially when it is used as synonymous for 'the social'. To assert that culture is central does not mean that everything else is secondary. When we consider the possible meanings, connotations and uses of the word 'culture', we face a mass of interpretations and symbolic associations. How are we to make sense of this concept? It is at one and the same time a mark of distinction and of the assumptions upon which such distinctions are forged. To study cultural things is an activity which often refers to the exploration of the practices and lifestyles of the elite in a particular society, of high culture, yet it can also involve the investigation of the lived experiences and representations of everyday life as in 'class cultures', 'ethnic cultures', 'street cultures', even 'subcultures' and 'club cultures' (Thornton 1995). We organize our thoughts and make sense of the things we experience through the rules of conduct through which distinctions are maintained. The choices made by social scientists and cultural researchers to engage in the study of this or that segment of a cultural hierarchy are made within the prevailing rules of conduct in which they live. The rules of conduct in social research are themselves classificatory practices. Social research therefore involves cultural agency (whether it is conscious or not) and this can reinforce or destabilize the conditions of existence of an object of analysis. Consider the shift within political studies from the study of the state as a *sui generis* object to a greater concern with civility, horizontal and vertical networks, globalization and transnational relations, institutions and movements. Indeed, the state has even been described as hollowed out.

The very processes whereby people study people are bound to raise this kind of issue. Since we can never be separate from the things we study (the system of language and specific cultural values, the rules of conduct and the established social practices, the institutional and textual conditions of knowledge production and so on), then the best position we can maintain is to acknowledge this condition and try to be aware of the way we draw upon and articulate systems of classification in order to engage in classificatory practices (the location of things in categories). In a discussion of the role of categories such as high, low, mass, elite and popular culture, Pierre Bourdieu (1984) argues that 'taste classifies the classifier'. In social science, the attachment to markers of authenticity, like validity, reliability, rationality, truth, progress and so on, raises the same kind of issues. Cultural hierarchies enable us to make a judgement about what is good or poor art. So too social science has its carefully maintained stable reference points through which we can spot an 'authoritative' piece of work, one which speaks in the appropriate voice. Many of these markers work through style and terminology, a rhetorical formula instantly recognizable through the subtext – which whispers 'I am true, believe me'. The distinctions that operate within knowledge construction serve as a measure of all that is considered to be worthwhile.

This means that the production and consumption of social research involves a dialogue between readers and writers, involving the cultural politics of knowledge construction, a politics based on the contradictory principles of trust and contestation. In addition, this political dimension indicates how power relations are an inherent part of the way social scientific practice is conducted. The kinds of knowledge produced through the social sciences operate through the normalizing and pathologizing of different kinds of behaviour and identities. If power is defined in terms of its consequences (even if we just concentrate on gender and ethnicity), then social scientific knowledge has a lot to answer for. The presence of social prejudice in social research is well documented but perhaps more significant is the way social scientific practice can be androcentric or ethnocentric (Harding 1986; Hewitt and Owusu-Bempah 1994; Guillaumin 1995; Richards 1997). We shall start by thinking about how cultural meanings are part of the processes involved in classification. Social scientific practices which embody received wisdom and cultural knowledge mimic the 'authoritative voice'; they embody the cultural heritage of a particular time and place for a specific audience. In this sense, the processes of communication through which the social sciences have come to be established involve a kind of performance which conveys meaning to specific audiences who possesses at least some of the skills to decode the messages, ritual and symbolism involved.

Consider the close relationship between 'culture' and 'civilization' which was established within Enlightenment thought and has done so much to legitimize the search for perfect answers. Many of the associations between the culture and the historically and socially specific logics of western societies were developed through the oppositions that emerged as a result of encounters with other cultures, in particular with the indigenous peoples of the New World. However, this had been rehearsed for centuries before through the construction of 'oriental' figures in the literary imagination of European writers. As a result, European societies could understand their conquest of the rest of the world as a cultivating process. If we trace the role of oppositions like those of culture/nature, masculine/feminine, civilization/barbarism, reason/emotion, same/other, it is possible to see how these were articulated together to construct complex identities. We make sense of identities not by listing their attributes but through the relations between insiders and outsiders, by asking the question do I/they belong? Therefore, we should be especially careful to take account of the procedures we have developed for making judgements about where such boundaries should be placed. The variety of ways in which social scientists have defined poverty and/or the underclass are not just the product of technical judgements in data analysis. They involve complex representations of the marginalized and the excluded, and articulate moral values. The fact that social scientists devise the concepts involved (perhaps with a little help from dietitians, civil servants and policy oriented pressure groups) should not mislead us; the academic debates over primary and secondary and absolute and relative poverty, as with every measure the researchers devise, are all politically charged and represent cultural values in a specific society at a particular point in time.

Judgement and values

If we briefly focus on the writings of Enlightenment philosophers
we can find ample evidence of the close connections between the
cultural meanings at work in European societies and the endorsement of the search for truth. In Kant's exploration of judgement
and reason we can see something of the processes through which
'cultivation' in matters of aesthetics, morality and epistemology
were seen as emblems of the civilized individual. The 'civilized
man' was a figure who could exercise judgement but strictly within
the established modes of authoritative knowledge production –
with the capacity to make a judgement as to what is beautiful, good
and true. The critiques forged by Kant have the appearance of
standing on solid ground because, as Paul Gilroy argues, they were
forged through the 'raceologies' which mark European cultures.
Kant's endorsement of slavery as a product of the natural order
provided a convenient scale of social differences with which to
assert the superiority of those he judged able to exercise reason
(Gilroy 1993). Similarly, Rousseau's account of the grounds upon
which human potential can be realized is itself grounded in the cultural meanings of gender differences prevalent in eighteenth century France. The cultivation of manly and womanly virtues is, he
argued, tied to the maintenance of proper duties; thus Emile
required a very different education for living a cultivated life from
Sophy, who was not capable of exercising a judgement on truth.
The capacity to judge is a product of active participation in the
moral, aesthetic and epistemological communities through which
we identify the demarcation criteria for what is good, beautiful and
true (and, of course, bad, ugly and false). To understand culture we
have to recognize the way in which its meaning is tied to historically
and socially specific situations. This involves a careful analysis of
the practices and lifestyles of those involved and how people make
sense of their own conditions.

Many studies of culture devise complex ways of classifying cultural texts and practices and we can learn a great deal from paying
close attention to how they do this. The association of culture with
cultivation (like the relationship between authoritative knowledge
with particular forms of education) remains a feature of contemporary discussion. We can see this when we organize our texts, artefacts and practices into separate categories and give each category
a different value and status. It is difficult to spot the classificatory

practices in which we engage, so we shall start with a historical example familiar to anyone who has wandered through the taxonomic displays of the nineteeth century natural history museum. A useful example of the close connections between cultural classification and the construction of authoritative knowledge can be identified in the politics of exhibiting other cultures within Victorian museums.

We should also acknowledge the part played by early anthropology in the classification of ethnographic artefacts in terms of a 'march of progress'. Anthropologists tended to view the practices of different cultures with an eye to their place on the scale of advancement – with instrumental social orders of the west at the civilized end. This was represented through displays of tools placed in a sequential order from the simple general purpose devices to more specialized artefacts so that the audience could follow the movement from primitive to the complex. In so doing, the audience situated themselves at the top of the scale of advancement and other peoples lower down. Henrietta Lidchi argues that ethnographic artefacts were taken as the 'material embodiment of the socio-cultural complexities of other cultures' (Lidchi 1997: 190). Cultures were reduced to artefacts and, in turn, these artefacts were understood by their place in a raceological hierarchy. Their meaning came to be fixed through the systems of representation which provide convincing and plausible narratives of human development.

The interventions of ethnocentric anthropologists ensured that these representations came to be seen as a 'true' account of how western societies had emerged and how they came to be seen as advanced. Such displays were taken as a literal depiction of the identity of the other culture and their place in a pecking order, rather than a complex representation of one culture by another. Of course, whether they were read as such depended on the way the audience made sense of the display and their familiarity with raceologies through which cultural differences were given shape and form. The debates around the origin of the human species which predate but were also stimulated by the ideas of Charles Darwin provided a tangible opportunity for popularizing the idea that cultural differences were a living reminder of human evolution. This concern had been an important feature of academic debate about whether cultural differences reflected the different evolutionary pathways of the human species (the polygenetic account). Social Darwinist movements caricatured such accounts of species development so that they could classify the people within their own societies as 'evolutionary misfits' or as 'degenerate' in much the same way as early anthropology had classified non-western cultures. The consequences of this can be seen in the sterilization programmes in institutions such as the Lynchburg colony in the United States. By the early twentieth century raceological hierarchies were a common feature of popular encyclopedias and school books. In such representations, European cultures were placed in a privileged position over other cultures.

While it is easier to pinpoint the arbitrary character of classifications past (especially those which translate easily recognizable prejudices into fact), when we look at our own classificatory practices we face a problem. The judgement criteria through which we construct distinctions is so much a part of the way we make sense of the social world that they are often hard to identify. This is the 'conundrum of culture'; the very distinctions which the study of culture is supposed to identify are also the taken-for-granted common-sense assumptions through which we define and value cultural practices and artefacts in the first place. The classification systems which we inhabit have a shaping role on the way we define culture and the way we value different kinds of human activities. For example, judgements made about taste have tended to draw upon the Kantian formulation of aesthetic judgement based upon detached disinterest (Kant 1790/1987). This meant that recognition and appreciation could only be achieved through the application of a universal principle where beauty is attributed for its own sake rather than for pleasure, to serve moral purposes, as an investment or because it carries the sign of an established artist. In Kant's account, personal preferences or interests should never be the basis for making an aesthetic judgement. If taste exists at all then it must apply to all people for all time (in Kant's writings he referred to all men).

At first sight this implies that aesthetic judgement should be beyond the contingencies of different times and places. However, we should also acknowledge that Kant argued that the aesthetic (the critique of taste) involved 'reflective judgement' which could only be made through the exploration of the many forms in which taste is understood in historically and socially specific locations. In addition, when we consider Kant's account of art as a practical skill based upon theoretical faculties, we are also led to problematize the usual picture of Kant as grand theorist. He defines art through the analogy of communication – of speech through rhetoric and poetry, of gesture through architecture and sculpture and of tone through music and colour. So, ironically, the person held respons-ible for constructing a universalist analytic of the beautiful is also concerned with art as a cultural practice situated within specific conditions (where skill is exercised within the production and reception of artefacts). Kant was caught by the conundrum of culture as much as anyone else. So, in the end, just as scientists draw from other kinds of judgements in ethics and aesthetics (despite the rhetorical use of the fact/value distinction), so too aes-thetic judgement often draws upon the distinction between true and false art.

Warning! This site is under construction: 'natural symbols' at work

If we consider a more focused set of cultural meanings and prac-tices, we can see some of the implications of this. To do so, we have to be mainly concerned with what Mary Midgley (1996) has described as 'philosophical plumbing'. The ways in which we can construct different assumptions about the 'right' course of action and what makes a 'good' outcome can have important implications for our decisions and actions. All the approaches to the environ-ment are normative, for there is a close connection between how they describe and conceptualize the natural world and environ-mental problems, and what they believe 'ought' to happen to the environment. For instance, Adam Markham (1994) considers the meaning of pollution, historically a key debating ground about human impacts on the environment. It was in the recognition of pollution as a problem that we saw the concept of justice (and the accompanying ideas about what makes for a 'good life') closely articulated with ecological concerns for the first time. The impact of humankind on the environment has always had what Markham describes as 'an anthropomorphic edge' – namely, that any attempt to explain pollution is packed full of analogies, metaphors and connotations which attribute social qualities to natural things and processes (whether we see nature as a machine, a female entity, a system or as part of a mysterious and divine plan). Basically, nature is cultural!

The theological picture of the world held that all things were tied together in a complex 'chain of being'. In this way of imagining the world, pollution was considered to be 'matter out of place'. This view of life defined pollution as an anomalous presence in the chain of being or as a transgression of the proper order of things. This understanding of pollution was reinforced through rituals in the preparation of food as well as through rules which emerged to prevent contagion through the transmission of disease through food. 'Pollution' is a symbolic construct, which we understand through its location in a definite situation and its relationship to oppositions like clean/unclean (Douglas 1966; Meens 1995). In the context of science, pollution is often seen as the unfortunate side-effect of the drive towards material progress and one that is open to technological solutions identified through the scientific method. It is hard to convey meaning without drawing on a culturally specific vocabulary.

Meat can also be seen as a 'natural symbol' as Nick Fiddes (1991) argues. The cultural meaning of meat eating relates to the way we think about the environment. Fiddes is concerned with the changing patterns in which meat consumption has been practised and also identifies considerable changes over time and in different cultures.

> Foods do not intrinsically symbolise. They are used to symbolise. For example, when we are told that the cooked dinner of meat and two vegetables symbolises the woman's obligation as homemaker and her husband's as breadwinner . . . the food does not itself stand for home-making and caring. The values are respective gender roles, whilst the food is the medium through which that is communicated . . . Meat certainly qualifies as symbolic . . . since its economic and social importance is frequently greater than might be anticipated from its purely nutritional value . . . The unvoiced symbolic value which underpin meat's popularity today principally concern our relationship with nature, as we perceive it. In this way, changing attitudes to meat, as revealed by changing habits, may also be eloquent commentary on fundamental developments in society . . . Thus meat is more than a meal; it also represents a way of life.
>
> (Fiddes 1991: 41–5)

In western European societies, farming for meat has been a well established social practice for centuries. In the early modern period, meat consumption was associated with status, and the differences between the various ranks and estates were marked through distinctions rooted in taste. A person's position in a complex social order was established by the way they engaged in ritual and the way they were located in the prevailing hierarchy of cultural classification (that status was tied to particular social skills and forms of know-ledge). The more extravagant their eating habits and the finer the food, the higher their social status (excluding the ascetic lifestyles of specific groups like puritans and monks). This had unfortunate side-effects in health terms. For example, the excessive meat eating of the aristocracy led to terrible bowel problems, compared to peasants who 'passed stools like cow pats'. However, the growth of meat eating has been tied to the emergence of a sequence of aspiring classes or groups in the social hierarchy over the past two centuries. More recently, meat has been increasingly classified in terms of its place in healthy and unhealthy lifestyles. Nevertheless, 'red meat' is still associated with passion and romance as well as conceptions of aggressive masculinity. As a result, cultural meanings will always contain value assumptions whether they are positive or negative (a judgement which will, in any case, depend on our own values).

The way we interpret the relationship between society and the natural world offers a convenient illustration. In environmental dis-cussions, there are two broad ways of thinking about the way human beings value nature: either streams, rivers, lakes, trees, forests, mountains and ecosystems are 'ends in themselves' or else they are a 'means to some other (human) ends'. Supporters of the former viewpoint (who argue that natural objects have an intrinsic value in some way independent of human needs and interests) argue that what remains of the wild places should be set aside from human use. For preservationist writers like John Muir (1901), places of natural beauty were not only fast disappearing, they should be regarded as 'temples', sacred places where people can replenish their inner selves by communing with nature at close quarters. The US federal government's decision to set aside Yosemite from development through the creation of a National Park, in Muir's anthropomorphic language, 'made the mountains glad'.

Advocates of the latter 'instrumental' view of nature are more interested in considering how natural places function for recre-ational pleasure or for providing resources for human projects. For Gifford Pinchot (1901), the wild places were still a 'resource' to be scientifically managed for the maximization of human welfare (to ensure that the maximum return is achieved for the minimum outlay). Pinchot's conservationism is concerned with identifying the most efficient means of achieving the goal of human progress. His attitude towards the natural world (that conservation equals development) and its utilitarian logic became established conservation practice. So, we can see two very different philosophies at work which demonstrate how quite different assumptions and values can lead to distinctive approaches to how humankind understands and treats the natural world (Smith 1998a). Muir's preservationist approach proved to be less politically appealing than the advocacy of careful stewardship and husbandry of Pinchot's conservationism. Development was both feasible and desirable. The pursuit of the welfare of both present and future generations were seen as linked, as demonstrated by Pinchot's adaptation of Bentham's maxim, the 'greatest good for the greatest number for the longest time'. According to this view, finite resources should be exploited but in a sensible and moderate way and with the minimum of waste. Muir and later writers like Aldo Leopold were concerned with the 'violation' of the 'natural order'. In *A Sand County Almanac* (1949), Leopold outlines the ways in which 'modern' urban life places a distance between everyday existence and the natural environment.

Identifying the criteria of judgement (in relation to scientific knowledge, ethics and aesthetics) is the key to understanding the writings of Leopold and Pinchot. In the conservationist approach of Pinchot, the key link was to establish closer connections between his conception of the 'good' (justice in terms of human welfare) and the scientific conception of the 'true'. Leopold, like Muir beforehand, ties the 'good' to aesthetic judgement on the 'integrity, stability and *beauty* of the biotic community' rather than just economic expediency. This does not mean that Leopold believes that beauty has no value, quite the opposite, he is suggesting that processes of valuation should recognize non-monetary factors (that knowing the price of something does not mean that we have established the value). When we value things, it is always difficult to separate judgements of the true, the good and the beautiful. The variation of such judgements across time and place indicates that they are the product of situated practices yet there is still considerable continuity. How do such culturally specific judgements survive the passage of time? We turn to this question in the next section.

The problem with cultural transmission

When we consider how specific assumptions and values are passed on across generations, it is usual to pinpoint the great foundational works of a discipline as reference points for our judgements. Canonicity should not, of course, be taken for granted; it has to be nurtured, reproduced and made relevant for historically and socially specific audiences. The survival of canonized works depend for their authority on the way they provide both a reference point and a standard for appropriate storytelling. Within the academy, these audiences (scholars, researchers, teachers, students and so on) have experienced a process of assimilation into received opinion so that they are in a position to understand the narrative structures at work. Whether a particular account of juvenile delinquency, welfare provision or the cognitive structure of the mind is plausible will depend upon the efficiency of discourses at work (whether they can regulate the production of meaning so that encoded meanings are recognized and accepted). The key mechanism for establishing the continuity of the canon is the establishment of a process of socialization where a standard is reproduced and endorsed by those who live within it. Theories of cultural transmission, which stress the importance of acceptance of the assumptions and values in the canon are a central part in the legitimizing framework for a discipline. Cultural transmission models have often been adopted in the educational practices of recitation and testing associated with formal schooling (Illich 1971). The assumption behind such models is that the audience are passive receptors with no opportunities for forging their own meanings, or at least of inventing meanings of any 'value'. This crude kind of model of perception was even described by Karl Popper as a bucket theory of mind. More or less implicit in such models are classificatory practices which assume that cultural forms exist in a hierarchy and that there is an unquestionable need to place things in fixed pigeon-holes (although they vary considerably on where the boundaries of taste lie).

Even more important are the ways in which elements of the canon become part of language, so that it becomes difficult to speak or write without investing something of yourself. If we focus on sociology as a field of knowledge, we find a long list of rejected propositions and arguments, breaks and ruptures indicating critical reflection. Yet, when we look at how sociological discourse is conducted certain elements are articulated repeatedly; so that specific ways of defining concepts, such as class and authority, are a regular feature in the formation of authoritative statements. Perhaps the most significant unspoken canonical figure in the sociological lexicon is Max Weber. Both in theory formation and in empirical research, the concepts, arguments and assumptions of the Weberian approach are evident: the use of the human imagination to shape experience; the generation of ideal types to give form and shape to complex data; the way causality and the criteria for proof are recognized; and the use of key conceptual distinctions. Weberian ideas are articulated with a wide variety of approaches from phenomenology to Marxism. Few would call themselves Weberian for there is little need to do so, the label of sociologist or social researcher does just as well.

The cultural transmission model has a number of flaws. Most importantly for a discussion of the meaning of culture, it treats the audience as a residual category and places the explanatory weight on the agencies which seek to embody and emulate the canon. In addition, it takes little account of the complex conditions in which meanings are produced and, as a result, misses the ways in which meanings and cultural boundaries are constantly moving. It also confuses how the agencies reinterpret past practices with the reproduction of great works. This persuasive model aspires to better things, to emulate the 'achievements' of the past and to pass on such practices to future generations. Yet it is fairly consistent in failing to do this. Advocates of the model are rearticulating elements of the past with new ones in quite different ways and these will be read in very different ways by specific audiences at different times and places.

In the same way, social scientists who impose their categories on the lives of people they study without regard for the lived experiences of these very people, fall into the same trap. The problem of cultural transmission can be seen by how we try to convince ourselves that we can do things in the way they once were. Perhaps the most interesting question which arises is why do we feel the need to invest in a canon and what this indicates about the motives for making 'authoritative judgements' about aesthetics, science and ethics. The simplistic account of audience reception at the heart of this model is tied to the way people are valued. The source of value is sought not in the lived experiences of those engaging in cultural practices but is identified in the judgements of those who are supposedly equipped to judge. The difficulty with hierarchical systems of classification is that when we value some things, we devalue others.

The fear of the popular

The area of culture most often devalued as vulgar, base and trivial is 'popular culture'. In defining a field of knowledge or set of practices with the label 'popular', we are already playing the classification game, we are working within a hierarchical system of cultural classification. The cultural transmission model takes no account of the ways in which the meaning of the word 'popular' is itself relational, that it is defined through its position in relation to other categories. If we define popular as accessible (or in a derogatory way as 'pandering to the lowest common denominator') we are working through its opposition to esoteric practices (or to the positive valuation of 'refined' cultural practices). Of course, this sort of distinction is very artificial and is based on quite complex processes of valuation which often only make sense when understood in the context of the time and place they were produced.

We can see some of the implications of seeing cultural classification as hierarchical by looking at literary criticism, specifically the cultural commentaries of F. R. Leavis, in developing the culture and society tradition of Matthew Arnold. Leavis argued that the survival of intellectual refinement and high culture in the arts, literature and philosophy depended upon definite mechanisms for sustaining the distinction between high and low (or popular) culture. In these approaches, cultural knowledge is seen as being transmitted through the 'authoritative voices' of those willing and able to act as the embodiment of cultural heritage. It was the 'critic' who acted as the custodian of all that is good and worthwhile in a culture. For Leavisites, it was the 'intelligent few' who should make wise judgements for the 'unintelligent many'. The role of custodian could only be given to those who possessed the ability and training for a 'discerning appreciation of art and literature' and were in a position to make up their own minds on what is valuable in culture. Leavis was particularly concerned about the effects of Hollywood movies in interwar Britain and identified a range of examples of cultural representation as damaging for 'young minds' (such as the Tarzan novels of Edgar Rice Burroughs). These kinds of arguments even crept into the social scientific accounts of the early twentieth century. In particular, Cyril Burt (1925/1961) drew upon them in his account of juvenile delinquency. Only the custodian could decide whether a text was a 'great work' and whether an author merited 'canonical' status. Everyone else, of course, lacks this capacity and should accept the second-hand judgements of these custodians. In this way, we can see a division between valuable culture, which should be preserved and passed on to future generations, and the rest of cultural experience which was regarded by this approach as shallow and escapist entertainment undermining the active use of the mind. This introduction will demonstrate that this model of knowledge is quite a crude one, for it adopts the view that people are easily manipulated.

For Leavis, the culprit was mass production and the standardization of both products and meanings in twentieth-century culture. In *Mass Civilisation and Minority Culture* (1930), he presents an outline of the damaging effects of Fordist industrial organization on the social and intellectual fabric of what we now call 'middle England' (broadly middle class and middle brow).

> Now, if the worst effects of mass-production and standardisation were represented by Woolworth's there would be no need to despair. But there are effects that touch the life of the community more seriously. when we consider, for instance, the processes of mass-production and standardisation in the form represented by the press, it becomes obviously of sinister significance that they be accompanied by the process of levelling down.
>
> (Leavis 1930: 7)

Of course, Leavis is not concerned about the lower classes; he focuses his attention on the educated middle mass who are being led astray from the righteous path identified by those best suited and trained to indicate a great work. His writings often focus on the effects of critics such as Arnold Bennett in the *Daily Mail* and advertisers (aided and abetted by psychologists). Not only did this debase the currency, but also it was a symptom of a general malaise. Leavis believed that he was witnessing the destruction of the social and moral fabric that followed from the disruption of local livelihoods by large factory based production and the 'dreadful consequences' of suburbanism. Leavis and Denys Thompson sought to restore the organic community from this kind of damage through their manual aimed at teachers for the training of taste and sensibility, *Culture and Environment* (1933).

> The great agent of change, and, from our point of view, destruction, has of course been the machine – applied power. The machine has brought us many advantages, but it has also destroyed the old ways of life, the old forms, and by reason of the continual rapid change it

involves, prevented the growth of new. Moreover, the advantage it brings us in mass-production has turned out to involve standardisation and levelling-down outside the realm of mere material goods. Those who in school are offered (perhaps) the beginnings of education in taste are exposed, out of school, to the competing exploitation of the cheapest emotional responses; film, newspapers, publicity in all its forms, commercially-catered fiction – all offer satisfaction at the lowest level, and inculcate the choosing of the most immediate pleasures, got with the least effort.

(Leavis and Thompson 1933: 3)

This rather simplistic model of advertisers and base critics undermining the standard and reducing critical appreciation to the lowest common denominator can also be found in the Marxist inspired cultural commentary of the Frankfurt School. This attitude towards culture is similar to that adopted by scientists who wish to establish their version of events as the most authoritative. In an era where mass communication and mass education have been largely embraced, it is hard to support the cultural politics of this approach to knowledge. In fact, this approach is useful in highlighting the connections between this elitist account of culture and moral regulation.

Culture, science and authoritative knowledge

Scientific texts and scientists in both the natural and social sciences can become canonized; becoming the measure of what is considered as valuable and useful theory and method. When social scientific texts and their authors become widely established as authoritative, it is worthwhile thinking of them in these terms. Most disciplines in the social sciences have their canons, whether this is Adam Smith, John Maynard Keynes or Milton Friedman in economics, John B. Watson and Edward C. Tolman in psychology, or Karl Marx, Emile Durkheim, Max Weber or Talcott Parsons (perhaps also Anthony Giddens) in sociology. When these writers and their writings are regarded as foundational in a particular discipline, then the canonization process is at work. They have become venerated points of reference for making judgements about whether a particular study, method or type of statement can be taken on trust. Of course, we all need operating principles to work from but we often fall into the trap of making a fetish out of our intellectual origins when we should be more critical. The criteria by which statements in science, art, literature and culture are judged to be of value, are broadly similar. Perhaps, we have become so used to thinking about the social sciences straddling the arts and sciences as separate and distinct domains, then we often overlook the similarities between them. What unites them all is the role of human judgements and the discursive conditions through which judgements are plausible.

Considering scientists (like literary critics) as the custodians of knowledge, that only they know best, undermines the critical and questioning approach which natural and social scientists use to justify their existence. This is, in part, a product of the contradiction between the dogma and the ethos of the Enlightenment. This embraced the search for a complete and infallible account of the laws of the universe while arguing that this can only be achieved through systematic scepticism and critical inquiry. Truth claims have misled social scientists on so many occasions that it is surprising that we should still hold such an attachment to their latest incarnations. Yet we still crave certainty and objective knowledge. Even cautious philosophers of science, from Karl Popper (1959, 1963) and Imre Lakatos (1970) to Roy Bhaskar (1989), who in their different ways see knowledge as 'fallible', are still paying lip-service to this quest for the holy grail. They are simply shelving the problem. To say that the knowledge we have can be taken to be true until falsified or until a better explanation of relations and structures comes along still treats existing theories as true in the meantime. Fallibilism therefore involves the deployment of a rhetorical device which fills the gap until the next heroic quest can be undertaken, rather like methadone acts as an alleviating device for the desire for heroin. Much of natural and social scientific knowledge still plays the truth game, so perhaps there are many more closet truth junkies in the academy that the current contestation over foundations and essentials seems to indicate.

Culture and Everyday Life: the Ordinary is Extraordinary

Once we recognize the way in which cultural meanings are not simplistically transmitted from one generation to the next, from master to disciple or from elite to the masses, then our attention is redirected to the question of 'how it is possible to understand the cultures within which people live?' The production of meaning can then be seen as a continual process of reinvention rather than the recognition and endorsement of messages inscribed in authoritative texts (a feature of both cultural elitist and Marxist conspiracy theories). In Chapter 1 we have seen how the meaning of culture is much harder to pin down than is often assumed. This indicates something more than the obvious tendency of people to disagree over the meaning of terminology. Culture is a 'suturing' concept: it indicates a space within which competing visions of the role of human existence can be played out, all of which seek to fix the meaning of culture. It also signifies the certain prospect of failure for any attempt to offer such a vision as an explanation of all things. Nevertheless, certain conceptions of culture and particular modes of cultural classification have come to appear as unquestionable in much the same way as knowledge systems (for an extended discussion of the rise and fall of many 'truths' and associated demarcation criteria, see Smith 1998b). In short, the concept of culture is an open window through which we can identify the assumptions, values and classification systems at work in a particular location. Moreover, how culture is defined can tell us a great deal about the approaches we consider in this and subsequent chapters.

The idea that the study of culture should involve the exploration of the representations and lived experiences of everyday life owes its emergence, in part at least, to anthropology and to sociological research practices who embraced involvement and challenged detachment. In particular, anthropology forces us to confront the obvious. By looking at the lived experiences of other cultures (western and non-western), their rituals, family structures, courtship patterns, gift relationships, the transition from childhood to adulthood and old age, and so on, we can begin to identify what is so distinctive about our own culture. In short, when we recognize that something which we take for granted can be very different, this immediately highlights the tacit knowledge and rules of conduct of our own experience. So, in this sense, the project of cultural studies is carrying on the unfinished business of social anthropology by challenging us to attempt to understand our own social existence. Anthropology directs us to the study of culture as concerning the everyday lives of a community, group or society.

Nevertheless, this does not account for the development of the idea of culture. According to Raymond Williams (1983), culture is one of the central 'keywords' in human knowledge generally, as well as in social science. It is not only that most of the central arguments and concepts through which we make sense of the world are located within socially and historically located cultures, but the very idea of 'culture' is situated as well. Therefore, restricting the meaning of culture to the projection of a single viewpoint or even placing limits on what counts as cultural knowledge (for example, the 'great novelists', 'serious composers' or 'the works of scientific genius') ignores a great deal of what is of interest to a social scientist. The role of popular culture appears to have been trivialized and occasionally denigrated. We know that something is open to challenge and that received opinion is in doubt when ridicule and derision are operationalized to defend the 'established corpus of knowledge'. The idea that culture is just transmitted in a monologic manner ignores the ways in which communication involves dialogue between the participants. Yet, the cultural dimensions of human societies are the most significant areas of contemporary social research. Immediately, you can see some of the difficulties in thinking about and understanding culture within the social sciences. So, to begin to make sense of these complex problems of definition and classification, we will first consider how the conception of culture developed by anthropology was translated into cultural studies and, from there, the social sciences.

Cultural meaning and the selective tradition

The relationship between social scientific knowledge and the every-day lives of people, their relations, their institutions and their ways of making sense of the world is perhaps the trickiest one of all to address. The history of social scientific knowledge should be seen as a series of detached accounts of the social order and its constituent parts. While social scientists have disputed the character and con-stitution of 'the social' they have one thing in common. In most accounts of the social for the past two centuries, the object of analy-sis has been kept largely at arm's length. Social scientists have main-tained the pretence that the knowing subject is in some way divorced from the social relations and institutions through which they acquired language, identity and a historically and socially specific understanding of their place in the world. So, the idea that social scientific researchers can be (in fact, always were) involved in their objects of analysis works against the grain of past practice. That is not to suggest that challenges to detachment have been absent in social research, as this chapter will indicate, merely that they have now come in from the cold.

One of the most important areas of social research which have worked towards the *death of detachment* has been the study of culture. To address this, we start at the interface between literature and the social sciences. If we take Raymond Williams (1961: 41–71) as the starting point, we can see three important ways of thinking about culture.

- *Culture as the ideal*, the embodiment of perfect and universal values (the best that has been thought and written) so that analy-sis is limited to the search for and discovery of such timeless values within the lives of artists and writers or their works.
- *Culture as 'documentary'*, in which human thought, language, form, convention and experience are recorded, in part as a descriptive act but also one of clarification where they are valued through comparison with the ideal, through reference to the qualities of the text in question *or* through reference to particu-lar traditions and the societies in which they appear (so that valu-ation is tied to some criteria for establishing its authenticity).

- *Culture as social, as a way of life* whereby it expresses the structure of feeling of a social group and therefore should be analysed, clarified and valued in terms of the (sometimes tacit) meanings and values of ordinary behaviour and social institutions as well as in terms of their place in art and learning.

These three accounts of culture are closely connected. The role of the 'ideal' is central although there are clearly different ways of thinking about its role in classifying cultural forms. In the conceptualization of culture as social, in terms of its context, Williams (1961) still highlights the role of careful scholarly analysis.

> Intellectual and imaginative works are analysed in relation to particular traditions and societies, but will also include analysis of elements in the way of life that to followers of other definitions are not 'culture' at all; the organization of production, the structure of the family, the structure of institutions which express or govern social relationships, the characteristic forms through which members of the society communicate.
>
> (Williams 1961: 41–2)

For Williams, the so-called 'absolute values' embodied by texts or practices, as the product of historically and socially specific conventions, make sense within the 'structures of feeling' at work in a tradition or society. Hence, there is a special role for social inheritance in sustaining meanings and values. This does not mean that values and meanings can be transmitted but that questions about the place and value of artistic representation must acknowledge the complexity of social existence. The most we can achieve, it is argued, is the identification of a *pattern of culture*. This is defined as 'a selection and configuration of interests and activities, and a particular valuation of them, producing a distinctive organization, a "way of life" ... a particular community of experience hardly needing expression' (Williams 1961: 47–8). The complexity of cultural texts, artefacts and practices in any given period poses immense problems for reconstruction. Indeed, this 'structure of feeling' only exists in the same way through the survival of those people who have invested their identities within it. For the most part, we are left with remnants, yet elements survive in an unpredictable way through the informal mechanisms of cultural reproduction and transformation. Any attempt to rebuild a record of past cultures (without living witnesses) remains an approximation, a 'culture of a period' rather than a 'lived culture'.

If we consider documentary accounts of everyday life such as those conducted by the Mass Observation researchers in the 1930s and 1940s, we can begin to build up a snapshot of the concerns in everyday life. Such studies can serve as important 'myth-exploders' in challenging received opinion about the past. For instance, the Mass Observation research on Britain in the Blitz during the Second World War reveal significant anguish, discord, class division and resentment, challenging the solidaristic impression prevalent in the post-war image of the war. The use of living witnesses to access the cultures of the past, such as in the oral testimonies collected and edited by cultural historians such as Steve Humphries, performs a similar function. Using personal experiences and tracing life histories, Humphries and Gordon (1993) demonstrate that blanket generalizations about sexual self-restraint and the characterization of the early twentieth century as orderly and harmonious present a simplistic and misleading picture of everyday existence. Interviews with former 'juvenile delinquents' from the 1930s to the 1950s demonstrate the extent of petty crime that went unrecorded in crime statistics. Similarly, the recorded testimonies of political activists and police officers indicate a high level of interwar public disorder which is absent in standard historical narratives. More often, however, such research can provide a vivid reconstruction of the feelings and concerns of a particular time and place. The following extract, a recollection of Hull during the bombing raids in the Second World War, provides an illustration of this approach to cultural history.

> Well the shelter was only down the terrace. We'd set off with three children, you know, two would be hanging on to me skirts, and I'd be carrying John. You had to carry him on your hip because he was so big. We'd be walking slowly and look up at the sky and you'd see all those flashing things. And you always thought it was nearly on top of you . . . It wore you out, you know, so that you'd no energy for anything, like. We was desperate for it to end. Then you see when you went out next morning it was shocking, people walking through all those great big hosepipes and old buildings aflame, and homes still burning.
>
> (Humphries and Gordon 1993: 222–3)

Accounts such as these can enable us to build a powerful image through which we can empathize with the experiences of the past. Another feature of research of this kind is the vivid way it can represent experiences which were once commonplace and now appear shocking, such as the sudden effects of life-threatening illnesses.

The next morning I woke up early and I could hear the most unusual noise and it was a man crying. I'd never heard such a thing and I got out of bed, opened the door and went and stood on the landing and I could hear my dad crying and as I stood there my auntie came along and she said, 'Dot, Rosie's very ill, go back to bed'. So I did and we lay there for a little while and I got out of bed again and this time I opened the door and I saw my poor mum standing there in her nightie with her old brown overall over her nightie and she wasn't dressed . . . and my mum said, 'She's dead.' Just like that. She said, 'Get yourselves ready for school.' And we went off to school and when I got to the infant's door I stopped for a minute because Rosie had just started at the infants and I usually took her in, but I thought I'd better not because if I went in and tried to tell them I would cry, and my sister always called me a watercart anyway, so I didn't want to cry in front of the teacher . . . After a while the headmistress of the infants came in and spoke to the teacher and they called me out to the front and my teacher said, 'Rosie's not in school today, Doris.' And I said, 'No she's not coming anymore, she's dead.' And the teacher said, 'Oh, my God.' Then I went and sat down. When I got home from school it was so quiet and then I realized that other days my mum was always singing when she got the dinner ready, but she didn't sing, and when Dad came home he didn't whistle.

(Humphries and Gordon 1993: 134–5)

After reading passages like this, once we have had a chance to recover from the obvious pain conveyed within such candid accounts of difficult and horrible experiences, we can acknowledge the effectiveness of oral testimony in providing powerful mental imagery of a time and place with which most readers are unfamiliar. In this extract, a great deal is communicated when we read between the lines. An underlying stoicism and acceptance of high levels of child mortality as something which was not allowed to disrupt the pace of life – the school day, the working day, the preparation of dinner. However, our reading can never be an innocent one. We make sense of such experiences by constructing imaginary figures which provide a strong sense of rules of conduct attached to gender roles. As readers we continually produce meanings in complex and often unanticipated ways. It also helps us to pinpoint our own assumptions about past experiences. We should also bear in mind the way that such accounts involve the selective judgements through which the respondents have processed their distant memories as well as the careful selective editing of Humphries and Gordon. There are various layers of storytelling at work in all such accounts. Nevertheless, the recollections of living witnesses can provide us with a very useful picture, one which is quite different from studying statistical information on infant mortality rates in the early twentieth century (when one in six children died before their first birthday). The cultural histories of everyday life at least help us begin to attempt to understand the 'structure of feeling' that underlies a particular culture and its shared values.

The culturalist approaches developed by both Raymond Williams and Richard Hoggart, despite reservations I shall address shortly, at least take popular culture seriously as a legitimate object of analysis for they acknowledge the rich variety of cultural forms. When considering the contribution of a writer as seminal and as diverse as Williams, Paul Willis (1990) successfully captures the importance of recognizing the ordinariness of culture (although in this statement he adds some of the vocabulary of Michel de Certeau).

> It is the extraordinary in the ordinary, which is extraordinary, which makes both into culture, common culture. We are thinking of the extraordinary symbolic creativity of the multitude of ways in which young people use, humanise, decorate and invest with meanings their common and immediate life spaces and social practices – personal styles and choice of clothes; selective and active use of music, TV, magazines, decoration of bedrooms, the rituals of romance and subcultural styles; the style, banter and drama of friendship groups; music-making and dance. Nor are these pursuits and activities trivial or inconsequential . . . they can be crucial to the creation and sustenance of individual and group identities.
>
> (Willis 1990: 2)

Of particular importance are the general processes of selection at work in any historically and socially specific location. For Williams, the survival of elements from a lived culture is governed by the selective tradition which provides rules of conduct for making judgements about what is good, relevant, useful and the best example of a kind of work. This selective tradition can be characterized as a multigenerational process whereby the organized system of values and emphases of a period are translated into a set of codes. These codes make sense within the terms of reference of the evolution of the tradition prior to the period in question and they can be articulated within its subsequent development. So, Williams is acknowledging not only the *complexity* of the objects of analysis within cultural studies but also the *uncertainty* attached to the rules through which cultural judgements are made (although such judgements appear to be well grounded in a specific time and place).

> The selective tradition thus creates, at one level, a general human cul-
> ture; at another level, the historical record of a particular society; at a
> third level, most difficult to accept and assess, a rejection of consider-
> able areas of what was once a living culture.
>
> (Williams 1961: 51)

For Williams, such selectivity is tied to the social structure and particularly the system of class differences which underpins it. As we
have seen in Chapter 1, this is a feature also of other fields of knowledge where judgements are made (such as science, ethics and aesthetics where demarcation criteria have come and gone with the
succession of academic communities). Moreover, it also helps us to
understand the relationship of Williams to the Leavisite approach
to culture. In the writings of Williams and other cultural commen-
tators in the 1950s (especially Hoggart) we can see the first attempts
to rearticulate the arguments and interpretive techniques of the
Leavisite selective tradition. In their different ways, both Williams
and Hoggart spoke the language of the Leavisites.

The culturalist legacy is a mixed one. The account of popular
culture developed by Richard Hoggart, consistently developed
from *The Uses of Literacy* (1957) to *The Way We Live Now* (1995),
differs in important ways from the contributions of Raymond
Williams. While both explored the relations between culture and
everyday life Williams remained concerned with the traditional
objects of analysis of the literary tradition, although he
approached them differently from the elitists in the culture and
society tradition. Hoggart, however, retained the Leavisite disdain
for the vulgarity and 'meaninglessness' of much of popular culture
but at least took the texts, artefacts and practices of popular
culture as worthy of detailed investigation and analysis. Yet the
concern that Hoggart expresses in response to the damage he
claims has been inflicted on the organic communities of English
life by American mass-produced cultural commodities such as
gangster novels and spicy magazines is plain to see. He reserves his
most disparaging comments for the sex-novelettes, magazines
which appeal to 'adolescents of below the average intelligence and
for others who, for one reason or another, have not developed or
do not feel themselves adequate' (Hoggart 1957: 252). Hoggart
presents circumstantial evidence by indicating the presence of

inferiority-complex advertisements offering readers the promise of better bodies and sharper minds. At times, it seems that Hoggart is more concerned about the increased availability of offending items like 'blood-and-guts' novelettes than their actual content.

> There has been a literature of sexual adventure for centuries; one thinks of Nashe's *Unfortunate Traveller*, in one of its aspects or of Defoe's *Moll Flanders*. There has been a literature of violence: there has been, on a small and esoteric scale, a literature of sadism and masochism. But this new form is rather different. This is not produced from a small and perverse set such as made their own use of the works of the Marquis de Sade. It has a wider appeal at its own level. It differs from the sex and violence of Nashe and Defoe in its ingrown quality, it is violent and sexual, but all in a claustrophobic and shut-in way.
>
> (Hoggart 1957: 260)

The associations Hoggart constructs between the popular and perversion are clearly a pathologizing strategy. Popular culture is devalued for its pernicious effects in breaking down the capacity of working-class people to appreciate cultural texts of which he approves. Such is the residual elitism of this left-Leavisite approach that he sets himself up as the judge of such texts and the 'general trend' of which such 'pulp fiction' materials are symptomatic. In the same way as Leavis, standardized mass production, in producing 'canned entertainment' and 'packeted provision', remains the culprit for cultural decline and youthful sloth.

> I have in mind . . . the kind of milk-bar – there is one in almost every northern town with more than say fifteen thousand inhabitants – which has become the regular evening rendezvous of some of the young men. Girls go to some, but most of the customers are boys aged between fifteen and twenty, with drape-suits, picture ties and an American slouch. Most of them cannot afford a succession of milk-shakes, and make cups of tea serve for an hour or two whilst – and this is the main reason for coming – they put copper after copper into the mechanical record-player . . . Compared with even the pub around the corner, this is all a peculiarly thin and pallid form of dissipation, a sort of spiritual dry-rot amid the odour of boiled milk. Many of the customers – their clothes, their hair-styles, their facial expressions all indicate – are living in a myth world compounded of a few simple elements which they take to be those of American life.
>
> (Hoggart 1957: 203–4)

The underlying cultural chauvinism is barely concealed and it is apparent that such cultural practices and artefacts offend his sense of traditional working-class values. By dwelling on the loss of clear markers for moral judgement within popular culture, Hoggart (1957) presents an overly romantic image of the rich textures of ordinary life, usurped by new cultural forces where it is no longer possible to separate the detective from the villain. This romantic conservatism and the moralizing tone is also present in his account of the forces which resist the influence of popular culture; such as self-help manuals on gardening and allotments, community centres, the Workers' Educational Association (WEA), local sporting associations, amateur theatrical clubs, brass bands, ramblers' associations and groups devoted to other simple pleasures. For Hoggart, the cultural practices of working-class life represent hard won victories to think independently and act autonomously which are now being dissipated by this 'spiritual dry-rot'. For instance, the WEA provides one way of fostering critical thinking and the demo-cratic spirit whereby individuals can make up their own minds about the kind of social and political order they would wish to see in place.

In keeping with the 'culture and society' tradition, Hoggart out-lines the close connections between educational and cultural prac-tices and the social structures of everyday life, the family and the community. To do this, he applies the techniques of Leavisite liter-ary criticism and cultural standards to popular culture whereas Williams (1961), drawing from social anthropology, suggests that we should study 'ways of feeling and thinking' expressed within cul-tural institutions, such as the mass media, as well as high culture. This type of analysis would also go much further than simply docu-menting the lives of ordinary people, for it also considers how it is possible to evaluate as well as reconstruct culture; recognizing its shared values as well as the ways in which such values are expressed (Williams 1961). In this way, it is possible to think about the shared experience of, for example, the working class or of people from a particular region. Later proponents of this kind of approach within cultural studies extended this principle to the study of the 'struc-tures of feeling' involved in the shared experiences through which we construct and reconstruct ethnicity and gender, alongside class differences. Whereas the cultural politics of Leavis was an attempt to defend the status quo and to defend the role of the custodians of knowledge and values, the cultural politics of Williams was to embrace the lives of ordinary people and to value popular culture in a positive way, as part of a project of a 'good life' for all people.

The attachment of Hoggart to Leavisite critical techniques and the preoccupation of Williams with literary canons in the culture and society tradition mean that they do not provide us with useful working models of the culturalist approach which can act as a guide to research. Better examples are *The Popular Arts* by Stuart Hall and Paddy Whannel (1964) and, within cultural history, *The Making of the English Working Class* by E. P. Thompson (1963). In *The Popular Arts*, a variety of cultural texts and practices from film, television programmes and jazz music are approached as legitimate objects of analysis although Hall and Whannel (1964) still attempt to play the Leavisite hierarchical classification game by making judgements about good and bad popular culture. They place a particular emphasis on the role of musical performance and media products as vehicles for self-expression and how the formulaic qualities of particular film genres like the western or the thriller can produce 'routine, banal treatments'. More promising in providing a picture of changing cultural relations is E. P. Thompson's (1963) exploration of the role of human agency in accounting for the complex cultural struggles through which the working class came into existence in industrial societies. This recovery of popular cultures from the past (a history from below rather than a traditional history of great leaders and elites) explores the contingent manner in which social consciousness emerged. This account of the formation of class identity was opposed to those Marxist histories which portray such developments as the mechanical products of economic forces and relations. Thompson also highlights the primarily academic focus of Raymond Williams' writings on culture and society and the disinterest of the culture and society tradition in classes, people, institutions and ideas in specific times and places (Thompson 1961a, 1961b). The study of culture from the 1960s onwards was to take much more notice of these things and, as a result, came into contact with the social sciences.

Culture and sociological analysis

So far we have explored how cultural analysis involves reading the lives of people in a particular way, in order to identify and interpret the social existence of the people under consideration and demonstrate how their values and stories make sense. This kind of approach contains a respect for ordinary lives which is absent in much of previous cultural analysis. In order to identify practical procedures for engaging in research in this way, exponents of cultural studies drew upon the well established tradition of qualitative research within particular branches of sociology which have since come to figure in a prominent way in other social scientific disciplines. The interactionist, phenomenological and ethnomethodological approaches within sociology also place a strong emphasis upon gaining entry into and having direct access to the lives of those being studied; to stand in their shoes and try to achieve a valid insight into their lives. These approaches also borrowed from research strategies pioneered in anthropology which enabled western researchers to begin to understand practices and the meanings of ritual in cultures without reliable historical records. In particular, they developed ethnographic techniques whereby the researcher becomes heavily and directly involved in the lived experiences of the group or community involved.

Interactionist sociologists initially used ethnographic research strategies to find out about those aspects of social existence which could not be easily explored through survey methods and statistical evidence. Research on sensitive and difficult topics such as criminal behaviour, 'homosexuality' prior to decriminalization and religious sect activities can sometimes only be achieved by direct and careful immersion (sometimes of a covert nature) in the everyday lives of those involved. By way of illustration, in one classic sociological study, Laud Humphreys (1970) adopted the position of voyeur-lookout in his study of casual gay sexual encounters while other researchers found themselves in difficult situations gaining entry to and participating within, for instance, gang membership (Patrick 1973; H. Parker 1974). Despite the time scale for such research projects and the intensity of effort, these kinds of studies tried to work through the relationship between the production of special scientific knowledge and everyday life. Participant observation, in-depth interviews and life histories (such as on the 'jack-roller' by Shaw 1930) have been chastised by the defenders of detachment for their open endorsement of the active role of interpretation in social scientific knowledge. Occasionally, largely because of the uses of these research methods to reconstruct the lives of the marginalized, these studies have even been vilified as the 'sociology of nuts and sluts'. The rhetoric of ridicule has been an effective bulwark for detachment. Yet, when we look closely at the way that such detached research is conducted both in the definition of the problems and the operationalization of research

methods, we can see a series of attempts to impose models, concepts and theories on specific objects of analysis. The outcome can
often be one-sided, partial, subjective, context-bound research
loaded with cultural values. Detachment has become a euphemism
for convincing an audience of the authority and truthfulness of a
study; however, it remains just one way of organizing and making
sense of complex evidence.

These interpretative sociologies embrace the subjective dimension of social life wholeheartedly in the research process and regard
the existence of objects of analysis as the product of our interpretations rather than treating such things as real. This does not mean
that such objective things have no effect, for if we believe something to be real, it is real enough in its consequences (that is, we
behave as if it does exist). In addition, they focus on the shared cultural practices through which identities are constructed and engage
in an exploration of the self, interaction and meanings. To do this,
they suggest, we should place ourselves in the position of the social
actor under consideration. Interactionism draws from the philosophy of pragmatism (in some respects, like Hoggart) placing a
special emphasis on the importance of generating critical thinking
in order to create and maintain an effective democratic society.
Pragmatists are concerned with the way in which meanings and
interpretations are the product of the 'pragmatic concerns' of
practical problems and purposes of social life. The mind is seen as
a tool for solving problems, as a 'thinking process' always in
development, rather than as a fixed thing.

Interactionism treats social actors and their small face-to-face
interactions as the basis of all social life. It suggests that the meaning
of any concept or idea (personal, political, philosophical or scientific) could only be located in the experiential conditions in which it
is produced. Hence the preference for qualitative research methods.
Practically adequate knowledge is derived through a process of trial
and error acquired through ordinary life in order to identify sensible
courses of action or modes of conduct. The self is not a rational cal-
culating machine but is a changing product of an ongoing process of
interaction between individuals and the meaningful interpretation
of unpredictable relationships; in short everyday life involves
informed guesswork. George Herbert Mead's *Mind, Self and Society*
(1934) argued that the prediction of the routine habitual practices
of others and how we respond in similarly predictable ways enables
human beings to participate in interaction and communication while

avoiding conflict. Through the example of the metaphor of the *looking glass self*, whereby other people act like mirrors for an individual's imagination, we can see how the individual imagines how he or she looks to others, how others judge the individual and how they react to the imagined judgement, so that we constantly monitor our own behaviour and anticipate the effects of our actions on others (Cooley 1902).

Yet, this still limits our analysis to observable social interaction rather than considering the unobservable motivations for engaging in interaction. It also ignores the meaningful relationships we develop as a consequence. The appearance of phenomenological sociology offered a way of thinking through the taken-for-granted assumptions that are usually ignored in interactionist studies of culture. Consciousness and the production of meaning are portrayed as the result of the intersubjective relations between actors engaged in mutual discovery. Alfred Schütz, in *The Phenomenology of the Social World* (1932/1967), argued that it is the condition of intersubjectivity through which the individual actors are able to grasp each other's consciousness and construct their life world. By sharing time and space, individual actors can engage in a process of understanding which involves the discovery of what is going on in the other person's mind (Schütz 1932/1967: 112–13).

At the heart of Schütz's approach is 'cookery-book' or 'recipe' knowledge; in short, we do not need to understand the origins of a particular set of practices in order to select the ingredients, bake the cake and 'eat and enjoy it' (Schütz 1943: 137). This approach attempts to establish closer connections between the second order constructs of social science and cultural analysis and the first order constructs of everyday life (Schütz 1953). By democratizing the production of knowledge in social science, this approach has close affinities with the way cultural studies has often attempted to challenge the role of the critic as custodian of literary standards. In everyday cultural practices we should expect that people behave in ways that cannot be anticipated by the 'fictitious consciousness' of either the scientific model or the literary standard. After all, critics and scientists employ the same procedures of typification as actors in everyday life, although the precise 'types' will be relevant to the context and specialized vocabulary in which they are used. The phenomenological approach questions the production of authoritative knowledge of social science in the same way as attempts have been made to problematize the hierarchical classifications systems of cultural studies. Yet understanding the problems in each of these fields of study is not, in itself, enough. To take this further, an alternative research agenda had to emerge.

In sociological analysis one of the most significant attempts to develop this concern with everyday life into a viable research programme was pioneered by Harold Garfinkel (1967) and became known as ethnomethodology. This combined Schütz's emphasis on the 'taken-for-granted' common-sense assumptions (tacit knowledge) of everyday life with the empirical research strategies of anthropologists and symbolic interactionists. The interactionist approach used ethnographic research techniques (such as participant observation) to attempt to reconstruct social life in a way that was as true to life as possible. However, they limited their evidence to the relationships they could empirically observe. Ethnomethodology seeks to find ways of locating and reconstructing the taken-for-granted common-sense assumptions of social practices upon which interaction rests. Garfinkel wanted to delve deeper into the lives of the people he studied and aimed to reconstruct the tacit or recipe knowledge they could not even express. In the ethnomethodological approach, human actors are constantly attempting to make sense of the mass of sensations they experience by drawing upon their stock of stories and meaningful interpretations. The moment that the evidence seems to fit the application of a particular story then the evidence is slotted into an existing narrative, transformed into a support for the story. This technique, the *documentary method*, involves a constant reciprocal process of interaction between the story lines and evidence. Consequently, the stock of stories itself undergoes renegotiation and transformation as identities are reinvented (Garfinkel 1967).

The documentary method also highlights how we come to recognize and trust detached scientific stories as authoritative. We carry a stock of tacit knowledge through which particular forms of knowledge production are recognized as authoritative. The vocabulary used, the object of analysis selected, the preference for closure (whether theoretical, statistical and experimental), the emphasis on generalization and explanation, the use of the fact/value distinction and the promise of progress and material improvement, all play a role in providing these clues. To challenge these taken-for-granted assumptions is a difficult task, but not a hopeless one. As argued above, narratives evolve and change and, as such, are contestable. Writers such as Kuhn, Feyerabend and Foucault have each chipped away at the established foundations of the belief in certain and universal judgement and, as a result, have in their different ways destabilized our trust in scientific judgement. Each explored the tacit knowledge at work in the organization of scientific practices. Some of Garfinkel's own research strategies also deliberately disturbed 'normal' relationships. They included the disruption of conversations to identify the rules through which respondents could adapt and accommodate such changes. A variety of investigations into the tacit knowledge of social relations have been conducted in a range of institutional contexts from religious movements (Bellah 1976) and casualty departments (Jeffery 1979) to the role of the police and courts in defining and processing 'juvenile delinquents' (Cicourel 1976). The focus of analysis, in each example, is the social and historical conditions in which a specific set of ideas or actions are located. This overcomes the tendency towards detachment associated with the application of natural science methods to social objects. In order to prevent social scientists imposing their own typifications upon objects in social research, a more adequate approach should seek to ensure that the concepts used are also intelligible in everyday life. These approaches have been developed by sociologists of science to reconstruct the 'structures of feeling' of scientific research communities, treating science as a collection of cultural practices and texts, as a heterogeneous terrain within which contestation takes place rather than as a mechanical process through which knowledge falls off the end of the conveyor belt (Latour and Woolgar 1979; Mulkay 1991).

Redefining the focus of cultural analysis

What kind of conclusions can we reach from this discussion so far? Any attempt to study culture had to break with the tendency of elitists like Leavis to disparage the 'popular'. The cultural analysis developed in this chapter also goes much further than simply documenting everyday lives but attempts to identify the extraordinary in the ordinary experiences of a social group or community. Later proponents of this kind of approach extended this focus on the 'structures of feeling' to take account of the shared experiences which do not simply rest on class differences. Whereas the cultural politics of Leavis was an attempt to defend the status quo and to defend the role of the custodians of knowledge and values, the cultural politics of post-war culturalism set the context for embracing and valuing popular culture, as part of a project of a 'good life' for all people.

Cultural analysis has been identified as an activity which involves reading the lives of people in a particular way. This involves identifying and interpreting the social existence of the people under consideration and demonstrate how their values and stories make sense. As an approach it attempts to respect ordinary lives, something which is absent in many previous cultural analyses. If we consider culture as a dialogic process through which meanings are established and transformed, we can recognize that words have plural meanings, that the ways in which words and ideas are expressed never belong exclusively to the speaker or writer but are open to many interpretations. Culturalists, anthropologists and interpretative sociologists open the way for this reassessment. However, they lack the theoretical tools for understanding the interconnections between the production and consumption of meanings. It is to the development of an adequate conceptual framework that we turn in the next two chapters.

3

Culture and Structure: the Logic of Mediation

Social scientists have always been interested in the place of culture within the general social system or, more specifically, with the interconnections between cultural and economic relations (less so about politics and culture). This does not mean that the issues of cultural classification raised earlier do not matter, for these will repeatedly surface as part of the story told in this and subsequent chapters. Indeed, cultural classification systems have been portrayed as a central mechanism for aiding the reproduction of socio-economic differences. This has been a significant area in social research, especially on the role of education in social exclusion. We will first explore those approaches who have maintained a privileged place for the economy, especially the capitalist economy, in explaining the operation of cultural texts, practices and artefacts. Theories of the place of culture in the social order has been profoundly shaped by the rise and fall of Marxist thinking and, in particular, the emergence of questions around the project of human emancipation associated with it. So in this chapter we will consider the materialist approach to culture and its role in relation to ideology.

Culture and materialism: Marx's legacies

The starting point is Karl Marx's materialist account of culture and society. We should tread carefully with Marx, for his writings have been interpreted in a variety of ways. The story presented by Marx and Friedrich Engels is an account of history with a beginning, a

quest and a resolution. Somewhere in the midst of 'primitive' existence, social organization emerged through which class divisions
were forged. Class structures are defined through the relations of
production; that one class, the unproductive one, extracts the surplus value of the producing class. This exploitative relationship is
taken as the crucial antagonism in each mode of production
although it takes a variety of forms in the different stages of the historical narrative. The causes of the transformations of productive
relations and forces in each stage of history (from antiquity to feudalism to capitalism) are located within the economy (the *base* or
infrastructure). Political, social or cultural transformations are often
characterized as a process through which underlying economic contradictions and conflicts are played out (within the *superstructure*)
as a more visible manifestation of class struggle. The operation of
the forces and relations of production in capitalism creates a polar-
ized social order in which intermediate social classes (shopkeepers
and peasants) are forced through processes of monopolization into
waged labour creating a proletariat which, if it became cohesive and
conscious, could transform capitalism into a communist mode of
production. It is this stage of historical development which Marx
believed would resolve these conflicts and contradictions. Commu-
nism is by definition the negation of capitalist social relations, the
absence of class exploitation (an unalienated existence). Three
brief features of Marx's thinking need to be raised to develop the
discussion. Bear in mind that the following key assumptions of
Marxist thinking are challenged by many contemporary neo-Marx-
ists, who argued that Marx's work was misconstrued and oversim-
plified by many early followers (including his close collaborator
Engels).

- *Base and superstructure.* As this is a materialist approach, Marxists argue that the economic base shapes the organization of the
  remainder of the social order (the superstructure) such as the
  politics, art, literature and the church. In Marx's ship analogy,
  the hull is a metaphor for the economy, the masts and rigging for
  the political structure, the wind in the sales for ideology while
  the philosophers sit in the crow's nest pointing in various direc-
  tions.
- *Class struggle and conflict.* The dynamic character of all modes of
  production is provided by class struggle. While a variety of classes
  and class fractions exist in a particular social formation at a specific

time, the fundamental conflict between the unproductive exploiting class and the productive exploited class can only be resolved through the transformation of the economy. In antiquity, slave owners exploited slaves, in feudalism lords exploited slaves and in capitalism the bourgeoisie exploited the proletariat.

• *Capitalism and revolution.* The capitalist mode of production differs from previous modes of production in significant ways. For instance, while pre-capitalist exploitation was achieved through extra economic institutions, such as state taxation, the development of the waged labour system meant that exploitation took place solely in the economy. The role of the state was to maintain the conditions for stable capitalist social relations. In addition, capitalism provides the conditions and the agents through which non-exploitative relations can be established, that is the 'historic task' of the proletariat. The processes at work in the capitalist economy periodically destabilizes the social order and, during economic crises, the proletariat is in a position to initiate change.

Within this materialist approach, human beings are conceived as creative creatures whose search for fulfilment can only be achieved by liberating their labour power from exploitative control. Much then hinges on the broad distinction between social relations within which human beings engage in useful work and exploitative social relations where this activity is useless toil. For Marxists, it is the institutional separation of non-economic relations from exploitative economic relations that is the distinctive feature of the capitalist mode of production. To understand the role of culture within Marx's account of capitalist societies we have to address the role of culture in previous historical epochs. In pre-capitalist modes of production, cultural relations were directly involved in extracting the surplus value from the productive class. In capitalism, exploitation takes place at the point of production institutionally separate from cultural concerns, like the rest of the superstructure. In this story of historical change, capitalism is unique in being organized in such a way as appearing to segregate cultural life from economic life. The mission of Marx was to attempt to demonstrate the close connections between economic exploitation and all those spheres of existence defined as the superstructure. Unfortunately, at the end of *Das Kapital* where Marx promises to flesh out these connections, the manuscript breaks off in a somewhat final way. His followers have been trying to fill in the gaps in this grand narrative ever since.

The logic of mediation: culture and ideology

The concept of ideology and its role in the superstructure are as contested as culture. Sometimes, culture and ideology have been regarded as synonymous. Institutions such as the family and kinship, education, religious and community organizations have, at one time or another, been described as mechanisms for cultural transmission and the source of ideological values. Ideology can be seen here as both a descriptive label for a set of assumptions and beliefs on how the social world operates and a prescriptive message about what it should be like. It is not hard to see how the terms culture and ideology have come to be used interchangeably. To recap on the opening sections, culture refers more to the lived relations in which we engage in routine practices. Like ideology, cultural practices are informed by values, and in that limited sense they could be described as ideological. However, ideologies are much more organized around a guiding political project, they can be assumed to have a greater coherence (with reference to founding principles) and they are often tied to the defence and maintenance of specific interests. Cultural practices are much more contingently organized, potentially incoherent and intersubjective. They provide a place where the many elements of our concept of self can fit with the fragments of other identities in a meaningful dialogue and enable mutual discovery. Cultural knowledge is unevenly distributed and widely dispersed throughout the social order whereas ideologies attempt to organize the social and political order towards certain goals (including keeping things the way they are).

It is only since the 1970s that popular culture, in the broad inclusive sense, has figured strongly in Marxist thought (with the exception of Antonio Gramsci and Mikhail Bakhtin who, since their impact came much later, will be considered in Chapter 4). So, to start, we have to look at the treatment of those areas and kinds of culture which are normally seen as higher up the cultural classification table (such as literature). In addition, much of the discussion about culture and ideology within the Marxist tradition has been focused on theorizing the relationship between class relations and cultural practices. If we look at the writings of the Hungarian Marxist, George Lukács (1957/1963), on the ideological role of modernist and realist literature we can see how this operates.

> For the realist school . . . Man is *zoon politikon*, a social animal. The
> Aristotelian dictum is applicable to all great realistic literature.

Archilles and Werther, Oedipus and Tom Jones, Antigone and Anna Karenina: their individual existence – their *Sein an sich*, in the Hegelian terminology, their 'ontological being', as a more fashionable terminology has it – cannot be distinguished from their social and historical environment. Their human existence, their specific individuality cannot be separated from the context in which they were created. The ontological view governing the image of man in the work of leading modernist writers is the exact opposite of this. Man, for these writers, is by nature solitary, asocial, unable to enter into relationships with other human beings . . . Man thus imagined, may establish contact with other individuals, but only in a superficial, accidental manner; only, ontologically speaking, by retrospective reflection. For 'the others', too are basically solitary, beyond significant human relationship.

(Lukács 1957/1963: 18–19)

In this short quotation, Lukács is drawing upon Martin Heidegger's ahistorical conceptualization of human existence as 'thrownness-into-being' as a tacit reference point for modernist literature; signifying that, in the modernist approach, it is impossible both to establish relationships with things or other persons and to specify the origin or purpose of human existence. In a well known illustration from literary studies, the Dublin backdrop of *Ulysses* then becomes irrelevant for sustaining the narrative. In this example, James Joyce's approach involves the construction of an examining subject exploring a fixed reality. As a result, he argues, these forms of literature cannot be used to explore human potentialities for these can only be adequately conceptualized in the concrete situations that form the backdrop to modernist storytelling. In short, modernist literature negates the outward material reality, portrays 'man' as solitary in an ontological sense and, thus, becomes preoccupied with the pathological (constructing nightmarish figures of perversity and abnormalities). This is an ideological device whereby modernism recommends psychopathology as a means of escape from the *condition humaine* (the experience of the brutal reality of capitalism).

For Lukács, who has some sympathy with the modernist portrayal of the human condition, the rescue of 'man' through psychopathology is itself the distortion. This rescue could only be achieved through socio-economic transformation. As a result, the modernist approach to literature, exemplified by the writings of Kavka, has often been regarded as a cultural manifestation of bourgeois class interests at work. Modernism prevents the emergence of a sense of perspective based upon an informed understanding of social context and the material processes of change. By contrast, writers adopting the realist approach must explicitly address the concrete (as well as the abstract) potentialities of characters if they are to adequately represent a 'truthful' account of their object. Unlike modernism, which assumes that human agency is impotent, here human activity is seen as offering the possibility of changing reality. Just as in the Marxist story of history, each epoch (or mode of production) is marked with a different set of material relationships, so realist literature develops typologies which suit each evolutionary phase. The contending literary genres explored by Lukács present us with a practical illustration of how he describes the process of history at once dynamic, contradictory, offering opportunities for the realization of human potentialities at the same time as putting the cork back in. Unlike many of his contemporaries, he saw cultural interventions as an attempt to represent human experiences as well as conceal the real causes of alienation but, crucially, they also perform a potentially transformative role within the 'totality' of social relations.

The question of the ideological role of literature, at least in Marxist terms, has often been posed in terms of whether culture is an instrument of the dominant class for ruling other classes (that those who control the means of material production control the means of mental production). Cultural representations can be interpreted as epiphenomenal manifestations of underlying class interests. Alternatively, in the proactive interpretation of this crude model of representation under the repressive Soviet regime of Stalin, cultural texts, artefacts and practices were carefully vetted to ensure that heroic proletarian sentiments were paramount. Moreover, examples of literature, poetry, architecture and music were proscribed for being contaminated by, for example, 'petit-bourgeois ideology'. Parallels with Hitler's campaigns against so-called 'degenerate' Jewish art, literature and philosophy, while offering little in the way of an explanation, at least point to the way that cultural representations were seen both as tools and as a battleground for political movements. Nevertheless, there is something deeply unsatisfactory with regarding cultural practices and representations as simply the epiphenomenal manifestation of unobservable class interests. For a start, it rests upon a simplistic conception of ideology, with culture relegated to serving as an 'opiate of the masses', as a vehicle for false consciousness which could be remedied only through the adoption of the scientific Marxist view.

Lukács begins to present a way of overcoming this treatment but is restrained as much by the Marxist lexicon as by the need to survive political vetting in the Soviet Union. For Lukács, the literary form involves a real and dialectical process of thought and existence rather than a reflection of isomorphic correspondence with class interests. Those representations which provide the proletarian vantage point with the total picture of the social order (or totality) could act in an emancipatory way. Those which fragment and dislocate our experiences (which prevent us from seeing the big picture of capitalist exploitation) are regarded as forms of reification whereby we externalize those relations which are a product of human creativity and regard them as fixed and definite constraints on how we can organize human affairs. Moreover, the emphasis on the commodification of cultural representations implied by this treatment of literary texts and the ways in which Lukács ties the discussion to the mechanization and quantification of all things in capitalist relations (drawing upon Weber's concept of rationalization), we can see a theme which was to feature in most subsequent Marxist thinking on culture.

The cultural industry

The attempt of Lukács to highlight the complexity of cultural mediation and the treatment of culture as a manipulative mechanism for ensuring the passivity of the working classes was endorsed in part by members of the Frankfurt School. This intellectual circle based at the Institute of Social Research was founded in 1923 but began to clearly develop a Marxist analysis of culture from 1930 under the directorship of Max Horkheimer. The collaborators in this intellectual project during the rise of Nazism, throughout their exile in the United States and on their return to post-war Germany, provided an interesting synthesis of Marxist social analysis and neo-Kantian idealist concepts to explore the role of culture in the increasingly mechanized and rationalized social relations characterizing capitalist societies in the twentieth century. For Max Horkheimer and Theodor Adorno in *Dialectic of Enlightenment* (1947), the development of social forces in both fascist Germany and liberal democratic United States was being shaped by the emergence of 'instrumental rationality' where creative and expressive feelings were sublimated by the remorseless logic of means–ends decision making and the functionality of tasks within a technologically complex division of labour. Culture, they argued was becoming commercialized and made formulaic in the pursuit of profit. Useful creative labour was being replaced by useless toil in all aspects of social existence. As a result, cultural artefacts became mass-produced commodities in the expanded market-place. Unlike Lukács, Adorno does not subscribe to the idealistic concept of reification, preferring instead to focus directly on the effects of material production on culture.

The adoption of the concept of 'cultural industry' by the Frankfurt School draws upon the way in which Marx destabilized the liberal assumption that economy, polity and culture are institutionally separate. It immediately pinpoints the interconnections between economy and culture and how cultural texts and artefacts are produced in an industrial process. The Frankfurt School, like Leavis, were attempting to make sense of the emergence of mass production and mass consumption. They also make a connection between the alienation and deskilling of labour in assembly line work and the value of the cultural products made in such a process. Cultural products, it was argued, were made in the same way as other items of consumption from soap to cigarettes. Unlike previous forms of cultural production where the artist, performer or craft worker retained some control and the product could be said to contain some form of originality, mass production had ensured that artistic and creative input only had value in so far as they functioned within the capitalist productive process. In creating homogenized, formulaic and undemanding novels, films, songs and documentaries, the standardized production system based on fragmented and routine tasks is portrayed as a cause of passive consumption.

Popular music is credited with producing 'regressive listening', discouraging the discriminating judgement which had become associated with high culture. On hearing a popular tune, Adorno (1941) suggests:

> The listener can supply the 'framework' automatically, since it is a mere musical automatism itself. The beginning of the chorus is replaceable by the beginning of innumerable other choruses. The interrelationship among the elements or the relationship of the elements to the whole would be unaffected. In Beethoven, position is important only in a living relation between a concrete totality and its

concrete parts. In popular music, position is absolute. Every detail is substitutable; it serves its function only as a cog in a machine ... In serious music, each musical element, even the simplest one is 'itself', and the more highly organized the work is, the less possibility there is of substitution among the details. In hit music, however, the structure underlying the piece is abstract, existing independently of the specific course of the music. This is basic to the illusion that simple complex harmonies are more easily understandable in popular music than the same harmonies in serious music. For the complicated in popular music never functions as 'itself' but only as a disguise or embellish-ment behind which the scheme can always be perceived. In jazz, the amateur listener is capable of replacing complicated rhythmical and harmonic formulas by the schematic ones which they represent and which they still suggest, however adventurous they appear. The ear deals with the difficulties of hit music by achieving slight substitutions derived from the knowledge of the patterns. The listener, when faced with the complicated, actually hears only the simple which it rep-resents and perceives the complicated only as a paradistic distortion of the simple.

(Adorno 1941, in Easthope and McGowan 1992: 213–15)

Adorno rejects the high/low-brow distinction as well as the distinc-tion between simplicity and complexity as inadequate for delineating serious from popular music. In serious music, the elements cannot be substituted or fitted into the listener's conditioned anticipations of what comes before and after the element in question. Popular music is 'predigested' and, above all, standardized yet it must also achieve the appearance of originality to whet the appetite of the audience; some capacity for change has to be built in. The process whereby music producers manage to deviate from established formats with-out disrupting the musical form is characterized as pseudo-indivi-dualization. Popular musical songs appear original but the inter-changeable parts have simply been arranged in a different way. Whether the analogy with machine interchangeability holds water will be discussed later. By way of example, in relation to musical technology, Adorno highlights the careful rules through which jazz improvisation takes place and how exciting variations and discor-dant or dirty notes become normalized by the listeners adjusting what they hear to fit with what they expect. The capacity of bands such as Oasis and Jamiraquai to recycle the anthems from previous musical types and combine them in a plausible way within the con-straints of the interpretive repertoires of audiences in the 1990s, offers a contemporary example of pseudo-individualization. As the

history of popular music now extends for half a century, retrospective musical variations or the recycling of riffs or a specific rhythm in
hip-hop reconstructions, where fragments of previous songs are
spliced together, have become the norm rather than the exception.
On the consumption side of the equation, audience members also
engage in strategies of selection and classification between different
musical types in order to regularize their preferences, maintain consistency and, from the point of view of the Frankfurt School, sustain
their inattentive and distracted frame of mind.

The motive behind this coordinated system of production and
consumption, Adorno (1941) argues, is primarily a commercial one
but it also has political consequences. The audience is portrayed
within the terms of reference of behaviourist psychology, as socialized to passively accept simple formulas and so becomes susceptible to authoritarian messages. Moreover, as another member of the
school Herbert Marcuse later argued, the advertising strategies
associated with mass consumption were responsible for generating
false needs in order to ensure that capital accumulation could con-
tinue. Marcuse concluded that the passivity and distraction generated by the cultural industries had actually ended the historic
proletarian mission of socio-economic transformation as effectively
as Hitler had crushed workers' movements in the 1930s (Marcuse
1972). It is the extrapolation of their experiences of the Nazi pro-
paganda machine to American commercial culture and the corresponding treatment of audiences as a homogeneous mass open to
manipulation which has produced most criticism.

In addition, as with the culturalist approaches introduced in
Chapter 2, the Frankfurt School widened the scope of cultural analysis by treating popular culture as a legitimate object of analysis.
Exactly how the Frankfurt School regarded culture is our next area
of consideration. When considering what was valuable, writers like
Adorno were articulating fairly conventional cultural distinctions.
Cultural classification is seen as hierarchical with popular cultural
products designated as having an inferior status. So, in the end, this
approach rested on a romanticized conception of the creative
powers of labour as a source of originality and inventiveness in cultural products. Bernard Gendron's (1986) critical reassessment of
Adorno's theoretical framework, specifically the concepts of interchangeability of elements and pseudo-individualization, demonstrates some of the limits to the framework and the analogy on
which it is based. Gendron problematizes the analogue of cultural

production as an assembly line. He argued that there are considerable differences between the interchangeability of functional artefacts (the product of the specific technologies involved) with that of musical texts. For instance, in the case of vinyl records, it was only after they were produced in the recording studio that they were subject to factory reproduction techniques in order to ensure their availability in sufficient quantities for the mass market. Thus, the musical production process cannot usually be subject to the technical rationalization (or even built-in obsolescence) that we can see in the production of, for example, the components of cars. On the side of consumption, for audiences the standardization of popular music can be seen as a source of pleasure rather than an attempt to conceal underlying ideological functions on behalf of the capitalist social order. The perspective developed by Adorno should also be regarded as shaped by the situated context of the writer both with respect to the derogatory way in which he considers the popular and in terms of his tacit ethnocentric celebration of western culture. The Frankfurt School remained captured by the logic of mediation, that it was possible to trace the role of underlying interests in the production and consumption of cultural representations, texts and artefacts. They also demonstrated that Leavisite arguments could be just as effective in the Marxist as the conservative tradition.

Structuralism and culture

Before we can see how the study of culture developed, we have to go on a short detour, by examining the influence of structuralism. This is an important step in understanding how cultural studies developed as a field of inquiry but is also essential for working towards the impact of post-structuralist analysis. In the space available here, I shall limit this outline to how structuralist thinking transformed our understanding of language. I will then consider the role of the concepts and arguments of French Marxist theorist Louis Althusser in paving the way for contemporary accounts of cultural identity and 'the subject'. This chapter will also emphasize the uses of the concept of 'overdetermination' in redirecting cultural analysis from abstract theorizing about the social order to more concrete analyses of cultural relations. Structuralism is, of course, responsible for more 'rolling eyeballs' in tutorials than any other concept in higher education yet it has still served as one of the most important sources of conceptual innovation in the twentieth century.

The structuralist analysis of language was developed in a series of lectures by Ferdinand de Saussure from 1907 to 1911, shortly before his death two years later. Since he always destroyed his own lecture notes, the *Cours de linguistique générale* was constructed by Charles Bally and Albert Séchehaye from the notes made by his few students. Appropriately, given that Saussure was himself attempting to grasp the production of meaning through the tacit systems of language, we have come to know about these seminal ideas only as they emerged through the interpretations of his audience. As a linguistic theorist, he was fascinated with the development of scientific knowledge and the ideas of Durkheim on each disciplinary project being oriented to a specific object of analysis, Thus, Saussure (1916/1959) attempted to establish the study of language as the 'science of signs'. He wanted to place linguistics on the same footing as the natural sciences although, indirectly, his work provides a basis for challenging the scientific characterization of the relationship between the study of the social and language developed by positivist and empiricist approaches to knowledge construction. The argument that language is a mere reflection of things, a transparent medium depicting the truth, is too simplistic an account of what people do with language. We cannot make sense of the spoken or written word without using a language system. In the construction of language, human beings assign a word to refer to definite ideas. This is possible even without speech, as demonstrated by the construction of sign languages through gesture by deaf communities. Thus, language is the product of speech and other acts of communication while, at the same time, it serves as the precondition for speech and writing. Language systems provide the often unspoken and unwritten rules that enable people to communicate effectively. Saussure provides us with a way of making sense of this system by exploring how words become meaningful through the operation of a tacit system of rules of language that enabled all participants in communication to understand each other.

Saussure distinguished *langue*, the underlying system of rules which enable us to make sense of speech, from *parole*, the utterances involved in speech. He suggested that this operated in much the same way as the rules of chess help us to make sense of the activities of the players. These rules govern the range of possible moves in a game and they provide us with a range of clues about the intentions and strategy of the player. Nevertheless, in language

systems there are no clearly written rules demonstrating the concrete existence of the structure of language, we have to reconstruct
this from the manifestations of speech. It was this focus on structured relations, that led to this approach being labelled 'structuralist linguistics' (Saussure 1916/1959). Of particular importance was
the distinction between statics and dynamics. Until Saussure developed this approach, linguistics had focused mainly on the evolution
of language systems, the development of words and their gradual
transformation. He was concerned to challenge the exclusive
concern with the study of change (diachronic analysis) and, in its
place, proposed the careful and systematic study of the 'forms' and
'relations' between the constituent parts of language (synchronic
analysis). To understand these relations and forms, Saussure
viewed language as a 'total system' (Hawkes 1977: 19–28). The
meaning of any word or utterance makes sense through its relationship to the structure of the language system in question. This
enabled Saussure to challenge the study of language as if it was
made up of discrete objective things (such as nouns, verbs, adjec-
tives and so on) which could be observed and classified.

Saussure starts with the images, words and sounds we use to
identify things, which he describes as signs. We often think of signs
as uncomplicated ways of communicating meanings. Actually, they
appear uncomplicated because, in everyday life, we already understand what they mean. For instance, if we consider traffic signs, we
do not distinguish between the image we experience (like a hazard
sign) and the meaning of the sign (in this case – take care, you are
in danger!). However, Saussure is interested in how we come to
produce meaning through signs. A *sign* is made up of two components, the signifier and the signified (Figure 1).

Within the sign, the *signifier* operates as the medium, the recognizable word, sound or picture which attracts our attention and
which communicates a particular message. The *signified* is this
message or concept itself. The process of communication involves
an act of signification. When, as matter of convention we designate
a word-sound-image to signify an object we are making sense of

$$\text{Sign} = \frac{\text{Sr}}{\text{Sd}}$$

signifier (medium)

signified (message)

Figure 1 The components of the sign

them through familiar patterns of meaningful contrasts and associations. Saussure argues that 'Language is a system of interdepen-
dent terms in which the value of each term results solely from the
simultaneous presence of the others' (Saussure 1916/1959: 114). It
is the relational qualities of language that allow us to understand
the meanings of words, sounds or images. In syntagmatic relations,
we produce meaning by putting words together in chains, whereas
in associative relations words can be substituted by another providing different links in any syntagmatic chain so that different
meanings can be produced. These associative relations can take the
form of synonyms (identical meanings) and antonyms (opposite
meanings, such as good/bad). Broadly speaking, once we accept
that words do not reflect the thing to which they refer, in the
manner of a mirror, then we are also led to reconsider the theoretical relationship between the signifier and the signified which
make up the sign. It is the existence of the arbitrary relationship
between signifier and signified within a sign that provides language
not only with its capacity to temporarily fix meaning, so that language appears to have a definite structure at any point in time, but
also offers the possibility that it can shift over time. On the one
hand, language systems are taken for granted by those who use
them yet, on the other hand, they are also reproduced, modified
and transformed through these very same uses.

Signification is also a process of valuation. Cultural values are
always at work when we describe and categorize what we observe;
when we classify things, we also make judgements about them.
When we give things a label, we also give them a standing, a position in a pecking order and an estimate of moral worth. We place
values on the things we talk about through the very words we use.
In turn, these words only make sense within the systems of values
we share within social communities. So, what does structuralism tell
us? This approach suggests that there is no simple or neutral act of
perception and that meanings are established through relations.
Every word we use to understand the world around us is packed
full of meanings and these meanings are organized in a patterned
way based on the underlying structures at work. Saussure thus provides us with some of the key building blocks for understanding the
study of culture in the social sciences. However, the theoretical
framework needed further development to be applied beyond the
realm of linguistics.

In the structuralist anthropology of Claude Lévi-Strauss, we can see how these ideas were applied in order to make sense of cross-cultural evidence. Lévi-Strauss attempted to identify the deep grammar of unconscious structures which underpin the representational systems through which we consciously communicate and organize our affairs. Like Saussure, he focused on relations organized in a system and the way that relations of opposition generate opportunities for change. Each element in the structure is defined through its relation with other elements although the total number of combinations is restricted by the overall total structure (rather like the way playing cards operate within a full pack of cards). Moreover, he believed that it was possible to pin down general laws in order to explain the patterned character of human behaviour in language, courtship, kin relations, exchange and the consumption of food. He drew upon the cultural analysis developed by Emile Durkheim and Marcel Mauss on the role of ritual as a means through which solidarity could emerge and common allegiances be internalized (see Durkheim [1912] 1976; Durkheim and Mauss 1963; Mauss 1990). However, rather than accepting that ritual has a specific meaning located solely within the location in question, he argued that the underlying motivation was a universal one. In this way, in *The Elementary Structures of Kinship* (1949/1969), Lévi-Strauss argued that despite the enormous variety of norms governing marriage, it is always underpinned by the incest taboo. In many cultural contexts, he suggested, the underlying structure of the Oedipal myth plays an important part in the regulation of sexual behaviour. What exactly is a myth?

> Mythology confronts the student with a situation which at first sight appears contradictory. On the one hand it would seem that in the course of a myth anything is likely to happen. There is no logic, no continuity. Any characteristic can be attributed to any subject; any conceivable relation can be found. With myth, everything becomes possible. But on the other hand, this apparent arbitrariness is belied by the astounding similarity between myths collected in widely different regions. Therefore the problem: If the content of the myth is contingent, how are we going to explain the fact that myths throughout the world are so similar . . . A myth always refers to events alleged to have taken place a long time ago. But what gives the myth an operational value is that the specific pattern described is timeless; it explains the present and the past as well as the future.
>
> (Lévi-Strauss 1963: 208–9)

Whereas Saussure was primarily concerned with developing an

account of the synchronic rather than the diachronic dimension of language, Lévi-Strauss described myths as moments where the synchronic and diachronic meet. Moreover, myths serve to integrate the underlying structure with the visible manifestations in everyday life. Structuralist analysis demands some kind of unifying mechanism for managing the contradictions of social existence in order to serve as a plausible explanatory framework for understanding events. Myths do exactly this. The distinctions between synchrony and diachrony and of language and parole, therefore, are integrated through myths. As you will see later, the idea of a hermetically sealed total structure or set of limits on the possible combinations of elements is open to question. Lévi-Strauss suggested not only that myths are at work in all societies but also that they are as rigorous and well organized as scientific knowledge. As a result, this approach played an important role in destabilizing the foundational civilized/primitive distinction and helped to destabilize the privileged status of western knowledge.

Finally, Lévi-Strauss draws our attention to the structured components of mythological narratives. In particular, he demonstrated how plausible stories are unconsciously grounded in binary or oppositional structures which work alongside the narrative structures through which a story unfolds in a linear fashion. The study of narrative structures is not new and can be seen in the painstaking empirical research of Vladimir Propp. In *Morphology of the Folktale* (1928/1958), Propp developed a practical demonstration of narratology within the Russian Formalist tradition in literary studies. His research arose from a concern with the inadequacies of study of folklore, especially the classificatory method which focused upon themes, motifs and names. Instead, he looked for an underlying set of principles which could be identified in all storytelling and found that it was possible to empirically identify similarly organized plots in many stories. He also found that stories followed certain rules which enable us to make sense of the various components involved. This made the analysis attractive to structuralists, for it reduced a complex web of narratives to a small number of rules or imperatives (which structuralists could later identify as deep structures or laws which are hard to spot on the surface level of appearances). The translation of the work misses important elements of the approach (the title should be something like 'The Morphology of the Wondertale', that is the adjective 'magic' is missing). He based his approach upon the scrupulous

observation of wondertales bringing together empirical observation with historical explanation. In Adorno's (1941) phraseology,
stories were standardized although it could in no sense be argued
that this was tied to the organization of production.

Wondertales were often predictable but were considered to be
much more pleasurable this way. In particular, Propp identified the
roles that constitute the character types and the functions through
which these characters act out the story. The number of functions
or moves is limited to 31 but the presence or absence of these functions serves as a basis for the classification of plots. The selection
of functions creates the plot sequence, a basic structure from which
stem the variations that work within all folk tales. These functions
and character types are listed in Table 1. The range of narratives
are grouped in four ways:

1 narratives that culminate in the successful completion of a difficult task
2 developmental narratives overcoming a long struggle
3 narratives concerned with both of these
4 narratives concerned with neither of these.

For example: once upon a time there lived a Tsar with three daughters; the daughters went for a walk in the palace garden (departure
of younger persons); here they tarried even though they had been
commanded by their father not to do so [violation of command];
the dragon kidnapped them [villainy]; they called for help [media-
tion]; three heroes hear their cries and set out on the quest
[counter-action]; three battles were fought with the dragon
[struggle and victory]; the heroes rescued the three daughters
[liquidation]; they return home; the heroes marry the daughters of
the Tsar [wedding]. This approach to narrative structure has been
applied to formulaic plots of Hollywood dream factory films, James
Bond movies, detective stories, thrillers and mysteries, as well as
television programmes such as *The Prisoner* (Berger 1998: 19–20)
with impressive results. It works especially well in the examination
of well established genres and offers opportunities for identifying
the connections between text and context by considering how the
film expresses and resolves the contradictions and dilemmas of a
particular time and place.

A popular illustration of how structuralist anthropology can help
us to understand storytelling in film is Will Wright's *Sixguns and
Society* (1975) which brings the approaches of Lévi-Strauss and

Table 1 The functions and character types in Propp's analysis of wondertales		
α	*Initial situation*	Members of family or hero introduced.
β	*Absentation*	One of the members of the family absents himself from home.
γ	*Interdiction*	An interdiction is addressed to the hero.
δ	*Violation*	An interdiction is violated.
ε	*Reconnaissance*	The villain makes an attempt at reconnaissance.
η	*Delivery*	The villain attempts to deceive his victim.
ζ	*Trickery*	The villain attempts to deceive his victim.
θ	*Complicity*	The victim submits to deception, unwittingly helps his enemy.
A	*Villainy*	The villain causes harm or injury to a member of a family.
a	*Lack*	One member of a family lacks something or wants something.
B	*Mediation*	Misfortune is made known, hero is dispatched.
C	*Counteraction*	Seekers agree to decide on counteraction.
	Departure	The hero leaves home.
D	*1st function of donor*	Hero is tested, receives magical agent or helper.
E	*Hero's reaction*	Hero reacts to actions of the future donor.
F	*Receipt of magic agent*	Hero acquires the use of a magical agent.
G	*Spatial transference*	Hero led to object of search.
H	*Struggle*	Hero and villain join in direct combat.
J	*Branding*	Hero is branded.
I	*Victory*	Villain is defeated.

Table 1 Continued		
K	*Liquidation*	Initial misfortune or lack is liquidated.
	Return	The hero returns.
Pr	*Pursuit*	A chase: The hero is pursued.
Rs	*Rescue*	Rescue of hero from pursuit.
O	*Unrecognized arrival*	The hero, unrecognized, arrives home or in another country.
L	*Unfounded claims*	A false hero presents unfounded claims.
M	*Difficult task*	A difficult task is proposed to the hero.
N	*Solution*	The task is resolved.
Q	*Recognition*	The hero is recognized.
Ex	*Exposure*	The false hero or villain is exposed.
T	*Transfiguration*	The hero is given a new appearance.
U	*Punishment*	The villain is punished.
W	*Wedding*	The hero is married and ascends the throne.
There are seven dramatis personae in Propp's scheme:		
1	Villain	Fights with hero.
2	Donor	Provides hero with magical agent.
3	Helper	Aids hero is solving difficult tasks, etc.
4	Princess	Sought-for person.
	Her father	Assigns difficult tasks.
5	Dispatcher	Sends hero on his mission.
6	Hero	Searches for something or fights with villain.
7	False hero	Claims to be hero but is unmasked.

Source: Berger 1998: 18–19
Reprinted by permission of Sage Publications Inc.

Propp together to explore the binary and narrative structures of westerns. In this study, Wright identifies 16 narrative functions which have featured in the classic western film. The functions are as follows: the hero enters the group or community; the hero is an unknown stranger; the hero has exceptional ability; the exceptionality of the hero is recognized; community still does not accept the hero; villains conflict with the community; villains demonstrate that they are more powerful than the community; a special relationship or tie exists between a villain and the hero; community is threatened by the villains; hero seeks to avoid conflict with the villains; a friend of the hero is threatened by the villain; the hero and villain fight; hero triumphs over the villain; the community is secure; the community accepts or celebrates the hero; and (finally) the special status of the hero is lost or renounced. Wright integrates this concern to outline the functions of the narrative structure with an analysis of deep structures corresponding to those identified by Lévi-Strauss. The standardization of the plots of classic westerns was necessary for the audience to develop a sense of familiarity. According to Wright, the oppositional or binary structures are the tacit organizing principles through which the audiences made sense of and derived pleasure from these films.

Any text can be analysed as if it were a language, that is that it was governed by rules whose consistency was established by an underlying grammar. In the case of the genre of the classic western, the binaries consist of good/bad, strength/weakness, inside/outside society and civilization/wilderness. The most familiar narrative, of a stranger intervening and then riding off into the sunset, rescuing the community by overcoming villainy and the primitive wilderness, offered a reassuring assertion of the memory of individualistic 'frontiersmanship' in American culture just when this no longer served as an accurate description. The contradictions of an increasingly industrial, urbanized and impersonal collective existence with a civil society which celebrated the virtues of individualism were becoming very apparent. The particularistic customs and values of small 'free-farmer' communities which were credited with developing civic and political culture in the United States no longer matched real life in the remotest sense. Moreover, the effects of the depression and the crisis of confidence in corporate capitalism were such that audiences found comfort in these films from the vagaries of market conditions and mass unemployment. For Wright (1975), the mythologies of westerns served to imaginarily reconcile antagonisms and resolve tensions. He went further to suggest that the evolution of western genres provides us with vital clues for understanding the social conditions within which identities are forged. Subsequently, in the 'professional westerns' that prevailed in the 1960s and 1970s, the hero is shifted into the wilderness to resist the evil and corrupt forces at work in civilized communities, so that the relationship between the binary oppositions has changed with corresponding alterations in the narrative structures.

Clearly, this approach provides a more adequate understanding of the complexity of cultural production compared to the Frankfurt School view of the cultural industries, yet two weaknesses stand out. First, the focus on standardization of cultural products (in this example of film genres) can lead the researcher to ignore the innovative and diverse examples of texts, artefacts and practices which don't fit in with the established canon. Adorno produces a very partial account of the diverse forms of cultural consumption in a specific location. Second, it also treats audiences and the character of their consumption in a crudely determined way. Even though there is some acknowledgement that the audience actively enjoy standardized cultural products and derive some pleasure from the twists and adaptations of popular genres (including genre-bending innovations such as cookery competitions and participative DIY programmes), the overall impression is of an audience of cultural dopes. In short, consumption is treated as subservient to production and meanings are assumed to be already inscribed in the text rather than produced by the audience.

Inventing the subject

Despite these weaknesses, and the next thinker to be considered has often been associated with all of them, a great deal of the conceptual vocabulary of structuralism has survived into recent cultural analysis. Louis Althusser gets a bad press both as a result of the tragedies of his personal life and from the caricatures of his theorizing which have occupied many texts since the 1970s. Therefore, in this deliberately sympathetic treatment, we focus on those aspects of his work which have contributed to the social sciences. Let's deal with the caricatures first. Like Lévi-Strauss, Althusser was concerned to specify the total set of social relations and reciprocal interrelationship between the various regions of the social order (culture is subsumed within ideology alongside the polity and economy). Althusser's formulation of structural or *metonymic causality* presumes that the relations involved can only be explained by reference to the other relations in the system (Althusser and Balibar 1968). Within Marxism, this was a significant step towards seeing cultural relations as an integral independent terrain. Althusser was attempting to work through the failures of Marxist economic analysis in order to adequately explain the cultural conditions for the reproduction of capitalism. Hence, structuralism offered a way of avoiding many of the simplicities of previous Marxist analyses.

Althusser (1968) believed that while Marx had delivered a *general theory* of modes of production, a *particular theory* of the capitalist mode of production and a *regional theory* of the economy within capitalism. Marx's project remained largely unfinished. Althusser argued that at the level of general theory there remained the task of theorizing class-divided social formations, the state and politics, as well as ideology and culture. At the regional level in capitalism, there also remained the tasks of elaborating a theory of the state and ideology. Althusser and Etienne Balibar, in *Reading Capital* (1968), had fleshed out a general theory of social formations as well as attempting to clarify Marx's contributions to this grand theoretical project. The essay 'Ideology and ideological state apparatuses' (Althusser 1971: 127–86) constituted the start of a regional theory of ideology within the capitalist mode of production. In this essay, at the abstract level Althusser identified ideology as a representation of the imaginary relationship of individuals to their material conditions of existence. When considering the organization of concrete social formations, he suggests that we should focus on the effects of ideological state apparatuses (ISAs) such as the education system, the family, political parties, trade unions, religious organizations, civil law, communication agencies (mass media) and cultural agents (narrowly defined as literature, arts and sport). This would facilitate concrete investigations of the role of ISAs in functioning for capitalist reproduction, in conjunction with the coercive agencies of the repressive state apparatus. Yet the level of abstraction made the approach appear deterministic and the applications that followed tended to be simplistic, such as the idea that attendance at football matches provided the working classes with a valuable lesson in the virtues of winning and losing, softening them up for market competition.

Perhaps the greatest misunderstandings have taken place over the distinction between abstract and concrete levels. In Althusser's theorizing of simple relations at an abstract level (as with Marx's theoretical approach) general claims are made about the social order that should not be taken as literal descriptions in empirical terms. Concrete situations are made up of the complex combinations of many abstract tendencies, some of which cancelled each other out whereas others combined to produce specific outcomes. So, in concrete situations, the superstructure could and did act against the perceived interests of individual capitals. The explicit use of levels of abstraction enabled him to distinguish the *determination* of the economy, the shifting *dominance* of economy, polity and ideology (in each mode of production and its phases of development), and the *overdetermined* operation of contradictions in concrete historical conjunctures (Althusser 1965: 87–128; Althusser and Balibar 1968 *passim*; Althusser 1971: 127–86). However, in relation to the reproduction of capitalism as a system (in highly abstract terms), the state and ideology were determined by the economic in the lonely hour of the last instance. Yet, as has often been remarked, the long run never comes. Nevertheless, the history of the Marxist movement had demonstrated that in specific over-determined conditions, socio-economic transformation could take place.

Althusser provides a very effective description of overdetermination by analysing the Russian Revolution, drawing upon the essay 'On contradiction' by Mao Tse Tung (1937). Within the standard Marxist explanation of socio-economic transformation, the primary emphasis had been placed on the contradiction between the forces and relations of production and class conflict between fundamental classes both of which are theorized in an abstract simple way. However, in the analysis on concrete situations, he argues that it is the interrelationship between primary and secondary contradictions, antagonistic and non-antagonistic contradictions and the uneven development of such contradictions which produce outcomes in different social formations. So, in the analysis of the concrete social formation through which the Russian revolution took place (and bearing in mind that Marxists did not on the whole expect revolution to take place in Russia or China because of economic underdevelopment) we can see a catalogue of exceptional circumstances and a tangle of contradictions. In Russia, these included the residual contradictions of the feudal exploitation of the peasantry, the presence of large-scale monopoly capital in many urban centres, mining areas and oil fields. Together, these conditions produced a contradictory set of relations between the capitalist cities and towns with the underdeveloped countryside. The retention of a 'ruling class' from the feudal aristocracy alongside the entrenched elitist military and the absence of an organized bourgeois class (due to the transnational ownership of many capitalist enterprises in Tsarist Russia) were significant factors in subsequent developments. In the context of singular events such as the failure of constitutional reform and the dire consequences of the First World War, a unique situation emerged which produced the February and October revolutions of 1917.

The point of this illustration is to demonstrate that Althusser was well aware that the crude image of class struggle as a juggernaut moving through history is inadequate to the task of analysing the social conditions within which change can take place. The structuralist analysis that he develops is an attempt to theorize the operation of class relations and social contradictions so that the complexity of concrete social formations in historically specific conjunctures can be explained. For that reason, the analysis of cultural institutions as ISAs served to accommodate the changes in the role of the superstructure, specifically the growth of state intervention, since Marx's lifetime. This could then be used to explain the wide divergences in advanced capitalist societies in post-war Europe and North America. Althusser did not do this, which ensured that his partially developed account was then open to misinterpretation for treating human actions as controlled by social forces.

In the structuralist Marxist approach, we are often led to assume that the subject is passive (as a residual category with no causal significance). Certainly, the constitution of identities is one governed by the structural relations of the social order but Althusser's account at least addresses the motivations for the way we invest in subject positions. A subject position is an idealized representation of what we are expected to be. Examples include the subject positions of the effective manager, the good mother, the caring practitioner, the loyal employee, the dutiful child, the respectable elder, the congenial host, the successful entrepreneur and, perhaps not so positive, the persistent truant, the flirt and the heavy drinker. For Althusser, drawing upon the arguments of psychoanalytic theorist Jacques Lacan, the powerful desires that lie trapped and repressed in the unconscious can be seen as a key factor in motivating our investment in subject positions which are not in our interests. Lacan provides a linguistic reworking of Freudian arguments to explain how identities are forged through our internalized acquiescence to the expectations of others in childhood.

At the root of this theory is the idea of the split subject which results from the break of the mother–child bond and the recognition of the *mirror self* (where the child, on seeing their embodied self in the mirror, acknowledges their own subjectivity). For Lacan, we go through life identifying with the subject positions that operate in symbolic systems of representation in order to manage the sutured character of the self. Althusser argues that the symbolic systems of representation in capitalist social formations contain subject positions which hail us. In this process, which he describes as interpellation, motivated by the desire to unify our fragmented selves, we reply 'yes that's me', identifying with these roles which, in turn, help to ensure the cultural reproduction of social structures. He is interested in the reasons for the proletariat investing in identities which aid the reproduction of capitalism but recent uses of this approach stress how this could be used to explain the adoption of submissive subject positions in terms of gender, sexuality and cultural differences (see Chapters 5 and 6). This shift from a concern with class differences to broader questions of identity was part of a broader reorientation in social science and remains Althusser's most important if unintended legacy.

Towards the complexity of cultural representations

While Saussure had hoped to develop semiology (as the science of signs), it was through Roland Barthes' reading of semiological analysis that we can see how this approach to language can help us with the study of culture. In so doing, this has helped to redefine what can be taken as a legitimate topic of study in the social sciences. As a result of Barthes' exploration of mythologies, objects of analysis in the social sciences now include images and artefacts which are part of our everyday lives. In the cultural commentaries developed by Barthes in the 1950s, he considered how a word, sound or image could generate meanings for those who read them within specific cultural locations (in much the same way as later suggested by Wright 1975). In the early writings, he adopts a somewhat uncritical Marxist approach to the purpose of mythologies.

Barthes develops the Saussurian formulae in order to make a distinction between how signs operate at the level of 'denotation' and how these are transformed through 'connotations' into ideological mechanisms. A denotative act involves a factual description of the thing in question and operates at the level of language (the first order semiological system), whereas connotations operate at the level of meta-language, of myths (a second-order semiological system). At the level of denotation a table is a single plane of wood (or combination of planks to simulate the surface) with up to four legs or a central means of support. However, a table is rarely explicitly defined in this way. When we see a table we think of a place for work, eating, talking, meeting, resolving differences and possibly confrontation. According to Barthes, these new 'parasitic' signifieds (exactly which one depends on the context) translate the original sign into an empty signifier so that it can carry other messages, so transforming their meaning. By way of illustration, he considers the role of wine and milk in French cultural life.

> Like all resilient totems, wine supports a varied mythology which does not trouble about contradictions . . . it is above all a converting substance, capable of reversing situations and states and of extracting from objects their opposites – for instance, making a weak man strong or a silent one talkative . . . Wine is part of society because it provides a basis not only for a morality but also for an environment; it is an ornament in the slightest ceremonials of French daily life, from the snack (plonk and camembert) to the feast, from conversation at the local café to the speech at a formal dinner. It exalts all climates of whatever kind: in cold weather, it is associated with all the myths of becoming warm, and at the height of summer, with all the images of shade, with all things cool and sparkling . . . Wine is mutilating, surgical, it transmutes and delivers; milk is cosmetic, it joins covers, restores. Moreover, its purity, associated with the innocence of the child, is a token of strength, of a strength which is not revulsive, not congestive, but calm, white, lucid, the equal of reality . . . A strange mixture of milk and pomegranate, originating in America, is to this day sometimes drunk in Paris, among gangsters and hoodlums. But milk remains an exotic substance; it is wine that is part of the nation.
>
> (Barthes 1973: 58–61)

The tools of linguistics aid our understanding of cultural representation and artefacts. In this example, we can see how something that is a feature of everyday life in France is reconstructed in a manner which recognizes the complexity of its connotations. Wine is a part of the same mythology as steak. If something that is an ordinary part of everyday life carries a wealth of meanings we barely acknowledge then a wide range of texts, practices and artefacts are susceptible to semiological analysis. Semiology therefore leads us to consider new kinds of objects for investigation in the social sciences. Things which we often pass over as ordinary, such as the consumption of food or the messages in adverts, are very important for understanding social life. It also sensitizes social scientists to the problems and complexities of representation, both in the ways in which they conduct their research and the ways they communicate their findings. We shall return to Barthes' writings in Chapter 5.

Social scientists have not given these aspects of communication the serious attention they deserve, assuming that evidence from more measurable sources is needed. To conclude, we tend to take linguistic and symbolic systems for granted, but these systems of representation are, nevertheless, the conditions of social practices as well as reproduced, modified and transformed through the ways in which we use them. Earlier, I argued that culturalists, anthropologists and interpretative sociologists lacked the theoretical tools for understanding the interconnections between the production and consumption of meanings. The same could also be said for all the approaches developed here although they begin to flesh out a more adequate account of some forms of cultural production. In the next chapter we look at those approaches which enable us to move beyond the fixation on standardization as well as question the tendency to privilege the economy.

4
Culture and Hegemony: Towards the Logic of Articulation

During the emergence of the disciplinary project of cultural studies in the 1970s and 1980s, another way of thinking about culture emerged which attempted to embrace the study of the popular and resolve many of the difficulties discussed earlier. Despite the rhetoric used in promoting cultural and media studies as an interdisciplinary field of study, the pressures generated by academic ridicule from representatives of established disciplinary projects and the increasing emphasis on research assessment as a measure of success have prompted many in cultural studies to opt for the emulation of the disciplinary framework of the existing bodies of social scientific knowledge. The tendency to view the established corpus of research as a canonized set of reference points and retrospectively reinvent collaborative work as a manifestation of this or that school of thought are all signs that canonization is at work. Few working in Chicago's sociology department in the early to mid-twentieth century would recognize the descriptions of 'The Chicago School' as a uniform body of thought and research that we see in contemporary textbooks.

We see something of the same elevation of the diverse research of the Centre for Contemporary Cultural Studies (CCCS) in the imaginary figure of 'The Birmingham School' and the canonization of Stuart Hall. Surely, it will not be long before the adoption of the shorthand of the early and later writings of Hall or, even more suspect, that the culturalist, Gramscian and Foucauldian Halls are about to emerge. With this kind of development, we will also see increasing attempts to set ideas in stone as foundational principles; in short, the generation of authoritative knowledge.

One of the side-effects of forging a new field of inquiry through struggle against the prevailing leanings of the academy is the tendency to resort to disciplinarity. The movement towards cultural studies grew out of the New Left and other radical currents attempting to challenge the elitist and hierarchical classification of culture such as that of Leavis. As a result, the language of radical political movements from the 1960s and 1970s can be seen throughout cultural studies, as is the preoccupation with questions of power and transformation. It is important to recognize that cultural studies is itself situated and as such serves as one window through which we can trace the shifting currents of thinking. While cultural analysis had previously been fixated upon social class differences, by the 1970s age, gender, ethnicity and, later, sexuality came to be seen as playing a significant role. As with the study of class cultures, the focus tended to be on identifying the mechanisms for social reform and transformation of each particular set of interests. The common belief held by a variety of new (and older) social movements was that culture had been used to shape the desires and conceal our 'real interest' in emancipation. In each case, it was the standpoint of the oppressed which served to validate the analysis. Culture came to be a terrain of struggle for marginalized groups and, as such, became heavily politicized. In short, (dominant) culture is the product of successful politics. A question remained as to which oppression offered the most valid basis for understanding the social and political order. For example, feminist standpoint approaches had placed a special emphasis on the role of the family as the cornerstone of oppression and the source of all other master–slave relationships. Yet black feminism was just as concerned with racist oppression as with gender differences. The family had also served as a safe haven from and site of resistance to racism. In addition, black feminism also placed a stronger emphasis upon building alliances with men to challenge structures of oppression.

The important but simple realization that no one formula could account for the complex and diverse experiences of all people meant that the presumed objective account of social order upon which emancipatory projects could be based could no longer be established. This was earth shattering when each movement had grounded their strategies in the claim that their experience of oppression served as the root cause of the others. The absence of guarantees and the recognition that essentialism had operated as a convenient fiction completely transformed the study of culture. What we have left is the use of a conceptual vocabulary which sounds faintly New Left but a very different set of assumptions that acknowledge the complexity of cultural life. To understand this process and then trace how the vocabulary has affected the social sciences more generally we need to consider the development of cultural studies. As previously stated, I do not want to perpetuate the growing myth of the Birmingham School, as though this was the only game in town in cultural analysis. However, we do have to recognize the contribution of the Centre for Contemporary Cultural Studies as a catalyst, not only in working through the problems on cultural classification but also in exploring the production and consumption of cultural texts and artefacts identified in the previous chapters. The CCCS programme helped to carve out a space and so legitimized subsequent research.

Rediscovering Marxism's hidden past: hegemony and dialogue

Two themes figured prominently in the study of culture in the 1970s. First, the question of the status of 'popular culture' and a greater concern with the relational character of the production of meaning. Second, the relationship between the organization of material production and the role of culture in the reproduction of the social relations of capitalist societies. The most important breakthroughs in the Marxist analysis of culture at this time emerged from the rediscovery and subsequent translation during the 1960s and 1970s of the writings of Antonio Gramsci on political culture closely followed by that of Mikhail Bakhtin's and V. N. Voloshinov's work on dialogic communication. While Gramsci provided cultural Marxism with a way of rethinking the base–superstructure relationship and of seeing culture as a contested space, Bakhtin's account of dialogic communication opened opportunities for thinking about the role of the production of meaning in supporting or transforming a social order. As a result, it became possible to assimilate the argument and evidence of the growing research on media and culture which had displayed no concern to change or even reform the social and political order.

The current conceptual language of cultural studies (and a fair deal of sociology) was formulated in the 1970s, although the uses are different now. Gramsci's (1971) texts made an important contribution in this respect. These had been written in prison conditions under Mussolini's fascism and, in order not to compromise his capacity to write at all, he developed a new vocabulary to conceal the Marxist character of the writings. Most importantly, he theorized the complex relations between economy, politics and culture in concrete conditions of Italian society (under the guise that he was occupying his time by writing on folklore). Most importantly he wished to understand how fascism had triumphed over workers' movements in the 1920s and 1930s. Drawing upon Gramsci's prison writings, neo-Marxist thinking breaks with many of the key assumptions of Marxism which had been accepted as foundational (although they also use Marx's own political writings to support this): that the superstructure does not necessarily correspond to the base; that classes operate in alliance with or in opposition to other social categories such as the bureaucracy and intellectuals; that classes are fractured by internal conflicts; and that capitalism does not automatically create the conditions of its own demise. Gramsci reconstructed Marxism as a 'philosophy of praxis' by arguing that transformation in complex advanced capitalist social formations could only be achieved through the careful prolonged struggles of mass movements. These struggles to achieve hegemony (political, intellectual and moral leadership) are conducted in politics, culture, education and the mass media as well as in the workplace. This approach presumes that history is made through many forms of struggle rather than as a function of economic laws or the activities of a professional conspiratorial vanguard party.

Neo-Marxist thinking is therefore a 'Marxism without guarantees'; it acknowledged that revolution is not inevitable and that the working class is not necessarily the agent of change. It argues that the complexities of the social order, the willingness of the capitalist state to directly intervene in the productive process and the capacity of capitalism to regulate crises and ameliorate the conditions of the proletariat all demand that a more flexible strategy has to be devised if transformation is to be achieved. Cultural relations are no longer seen as an ideological mask deceiving the proletariat or pacifying them with mundaneity. Instead they are portrayed as a terrain of contestation where social forces struggle in a drawn out 'war of position' (an analogy which draws upon the experience of trench warfare in the First World War). It is this attempt by different classes, alliances and social forces to achieve 'political, intellectual and moral leadership' in order to win the active consent which Gramsci termed hegemony (Gramsci 1971). It therefore has a double meaning. Hegemony signifies the attempt to secure dominance but it also highlights the impossibility of complete domination by any class or alliance (for if that were the case then no transformation would be possible). But how could such a struggle be conducted? This is where Bakhtin's writings came in.

The idea that culture can be conceptualized as a dialogic activity, as an intersubjective relationship through which change can take place came from the Bakhtin Circle (named after the Russian Marxist literary critic, Mikhail Bakhtin). In a useful analogy of communication as a telephone conversation, Voloshinov argued that:

> A word is a bridge thrown between myself and another. If one end of the bridge belongs to me then the other depends on my addressee. A word is a territory shared by both addresser and addressee, by the speaker and his interlocutor.
>
> (Voloshinov 1929/1973: 86)

This approach also recognizes that words have plural meanings and that they never belong exclusively to the speaker or writer for they are open to many interpretations. For Bakhtin, meanings are constructed through dialogue. Like Williams in his attempt to outline an anthropological definition of culture, the Bakhtin Circle viewed popular culture in a more positive way, although they still drew upon hierarchical distinctions. In Bakhtin's account of the idea of the *carnivalesque*, popular cultural activities were characterized by excess, vulgarity and indulgence, having their roots in medieval folk humour. The carnival, and its legacy, creates in our culture a window for voicing the concerns of those usually powerless to make themselves heard.

> The suspension of all hierarchical precedence during carnival time was of particular significance. Rank was especially evident during official feasts . . . It was a consecration of inequality. On the contrary, all were considered equal during carnival. Here in the town square, a special form of free and familiar contract reigned among people usually divided by the barriers of caste, property, profession, and age.
>
> (Bakhtin 1984: 10)

These exceptional celebrations provided a context within which arguments and ideas, grievances and niggles could all be expressed in a frank and fearless way. Without the ritualistic norms of etiquette and the usual relations of deference, the carnival was the only time where truly human relationships could be experienced. The use of these techniques to generate irreverent invective and parody those in authority also created opportunities to change the way things were organized. It was the way in which Bakhtin identifies the oral tradition of the carnivalesque as a feature in the development of the modern novel that attracts our attention here. As illustrated by Bakhtin's consideration of Rabelais, Dostoevsky and Dickens where in figures such as Mr Bumble (the workhouse master in *Oliver Twist*) we encounter a multiplicity of voices which demonstrate the hypocrisy and mean selfishness of those who use authority to congratulate themselves for their own moral rectitude. He suggests that in the history of the novel, we can see a thread of this carnivalesque humour and laughter which mocks authority figures (which he describes as 'Billingsgate' after the coarse and derisive cursing of the fish-women of that market-place). This contrasts sharply with the monoglot approach of the Epic genre which, in seeking to close down all other interpretations and meanings, suppresses all but the authoritative voice and, with a moralizing tone, stresses the virtue of tradition. Instead of a monologue, the novel involves a heteroglossia, a multiplicity of registers or speech types within a language, which captures and represents something of the ongoing complexity of lived experiences (Bakhtin 1981). The novel is therefore polyphonic, it contains many styles and voices each addressing different audiences.

> The internal stratification of any single national language into social dialects, characteristic group behaviour, professional jargons, generic languages, languages of generations and age groups, tendentious languages, languages of authorities, of various circles and passing fashions, languages that serve specific sociopolitical purposes of the day, even of the hour (each day has its own slogan, its own vocabulary, its own emphases) – this internal stratification present in any language at any given moment of its historical existence is the indispensable prerequisite for the novel as a genre.
>
> (Bakhtin 1981: 262–3)

Bakhtin provides an account of the production of meaning which assumes that the contingencies of speech and the use of intonation are a crucial part of communication. As we can see in the writings

attributed to Voloshinov (but now believed to have been written by
Bakhtin), this dialogic approach challenged the strict separation of
referential denotation and evaluative connotation which underpinned the 'scientific model'.

> This sort of disjuncture between referential meaning and evaluation is
> totally inadmissible. It stems from failure to note the more profound
> functions of evaluation in speech. Referential meaning is moulded by
> evaluation; it is evaluation after all, which determines that a particular
> referential meaning may enter the purview of speakers ... it is pre-
> cisely evaluation which plays the creative role. A change of meaning
> is, essentially, always a re-evaluation: the transposition of some par-
> ticular word from one evaluative context to another. The separation of
> word meaning from evaluation inevitably deprives meaning of place in
> the living social process (where meaning is always permeated with
> value judgement), to its being ontologized and transformed into ideal
> Being divorced from the historical process of Becoming.
>
> (Voloshinov 1929/1973: 105)

This approach recognizes the historical and social situatedness of
knowledge and the way that language can be used to tailor messages for specific audiences in definite material conditions. As a
model for communication it also offers a very useful framework for
understanding how social scientific knowledge can move from a
monologic towards a dialogic approach. More importantly, it
acknowledges the point that received viewpoints and high morality
always contend with counterblasts and voices of resistance. Texts
are characterized as a terrain of struggle, rather than being categorized in the manner of Lukács according to whether they pro-
mote human emancipation.

Communication and the production of meaning can be identified
as an intersubjective experience of mutual discovery and, as such,
open to transformation. In the fields of the social sciences where
the authoritative voice is taken especially seriously, such as economics, Vivienne Brown (1994), in her exploration of Adam Smith's
discourses, argues that this serves as a means of creating a canon.
By drawing upon the contrast between 'dialogism' and 'monolo-
gism' we are drawn to consider their stylistic, figurative and rhetorical forms. Brown argues that the writings of Adam Smith are much
more polyphonic than contemporary social science assumes.
Rather than offering a foundation for the figure of 'rational economic man', Smith's writings on the economy are shot through with
culturally specific ethical assumptions and values (many of which

would problematize neo-liberal readings of Adam Smith as a monologue). By problematizing the status of monologic texts, where one voice always seeks to have the 'last word', we can begin to consider the complex play of meanings involved in theoretical work. These techniques provide a means of identifying the metaphoric strands which can highlight developing story lines in the works considered. Paul Feyerabend's (1978) provocative comparison of a scientific textbook from the 1950s with *Malleus Maleficarum* (1484), the witchfinder's handbook, provides a vivid illustration of this difference. The various parts of this reputedly superstitious and fearful text deal with the phenomena, aetiology, legal aspect and theological aspects of witchcraft in a pluralistic way. Although it argues a case effectively, it still discusses the various alternatives in a balanced and evaluative way. The scientific textbook, on the other hand, tries to achieve closure and shut down critical discussion for fear of undermining its function in the transmission of authoritative knowledge (Feyerabend 1978: 92). Brown is arguing for a heterodox economics which can accommodate the complexity of social scientific texts. Here we are concerned with how Bakhtin's writing loosened the grip of established models of cultural analysis but later, when considering post-structuralist approaches to culture, we shall consider how these arguments can be read in different ways.

Cultural studies was already moving in this direction when these studies became widely available. In 'Encoding and decoding in television discourse', Stuart Hall (1973) attempted to find a way of retheorizing the dominant model of communication in mass communications research. Critical of the behaviourist assumption that communication was a linear process, a one-way relationship between sender, message and receiver (sometimes with further stages of intermediaries), Hall drew upon the Marxist metaphor of the circuit of capital. In this way, he devised a circuit of culture which involved the production of value in a similar way to the commodified labour process characteristic of capitalism. The institutional structures, networks, technical infrastructures were a labour process in a discursive mode, while the audience reception was the cultural equivalent of realization. To be consistent with Marx's circuit, the discourses produced must be translated into practices if the circuit is to be maintained. Cultural production involves the generation of encoded messages which are drawn from the events, treatments and images of the audience in the cultural context, and are fashioned into a meaningful discourse (whereby certain messages occupy a privileged place). In the moment of reception, the encoded messages are worked into the structures of social practices by the audience, in turn feeding back into the production process.

This encoding/decoding approach draws heavily from the semiology of the early writings of Barthes. Hall considers any asymmetries between encoding and decoding (the failure to establish relations of equivalence between producers and consumers of communication) as a possible source of misunderstanding. Different audiences also read the messages in different ways, depending on their taken for granted common-sense knowledge (a phenomenological point). Three kinds of decoding strategies are pinpointed. For much of the audience who have been socialized into the 'dominant-hegemonic position', they are likely to decode many of the preferred meanings of the dominant cultural order in the way intended. Of course, the local situations of specific social groups may lead an audience to feel that the preferred meanings are not relevant to their experiences – the 'negotiated position' somewhere between assent and opposition bends the meanings of the text. The example provided is that of workers agreeing with political messages in the news that sectional demands should not undermine the national interest and that this need not prevent them from engaging in union action themselves. When the audience produce a contrary response from that intended, they are reinterpreting the representations within an alternative frame of reference – an 'oppositional code'. The development of this framework by David Morley (1980) in *The Nationwide Audience* explored how different groups of people used their own experience to accept, refract or reject the encoded messages of an evening current affairs programme. The decoding strategies of bank managers, schoolboys and apprentices assented to the intended messages while trade union officials, photography students and university arts students found ways of negotiating the messages. These responses clearly differed from the oppositional decoding by union shop stewards and black further education students who saw little of relevance to their experiences in the programme in question. This study of audience responses is now considered a seminal one in bringing together cultural and media studies. In addition, Colin Sparks (1996) suggests that it kick-started the use of ethnographic research methods in audience studies.

Culture goes political: the culturalist agenda meets the neo-Gramscian project

It was in the collaborative work of the Centre for Cultural Studies (CCCS) from the 1960s through to the early 1980s that contemporary cultural analysis was forged. Initially under the directorship of Richard Hoggart, the CCCS went on to develop the culturalist research agenda of studying working-class culture, education and adolescence. With Hoggart's departure to UNESCO and Stuart Hall's succession to the coordinating role in the Centre, this research agenda was developed within the context of the account of hegemony advocated by the New Left (an intellectual movement, of which Hall was a part, attempting to apply Marxist and socialist arguments to the study of western European societies). By the end of the 1960s, the post-war consensus was effectively over and social conflict was an increasingly visible feature of British society. In this context, with Labour and conservative governments lined up against organized union activity as well as new social movements, the Marxist theory of class division and struggle was given a new lease of life.

To understand the work of the CCCS we need to situate it in the crisis of post-war capitalism and the fragmentation of support for state policies by organized labour and capital. In addition, in the 1970s, a political crisis emerged whereby Britain was seen as ungovernable. Public sector spending was subject to severe restraint at the same time as economic stagflation and rising unemployment had significant effects on the cultural landscape. A resurgent right alternative emerged which sought to restore free market competition and deregulation, drawing on the assumptions of neo-liberalism. The studies of the centre represent the cultural and political effects of these changes within the rubric of the cultural theories identified throughout the book. Structuralist arguments provided a framework for charting the effects of the capitalist system and emphasizing the role of culture, along with education, in reproducing capitalism as a system. In acknowledging the mistakes of previous generations of Marxist inspired theorists they rejected economic determinism. Instead, they concentrated on economic, political and ideological strategies through which hegemonic projects were constructed. This placed a greater emphasis upon the role of strategic agents or forces in concrete overdetermined conditions rather than social structures theorized in more abstract terms.

The research environment of the CCCS was ad hoc, interdisciplinary and intensely collaborative and this shaped the form of cultural research and theorizing. The approaches adopted were eclectic and synthetic as well as concerned with topical controversial issues such as emerging youth subcultures and disaffection, cultural stereotyping in the mass media, and the policing of ethnic minorities. In this brief account, three studies associated with the CCCS will be highlighted. In *Resistance through Rituals* (Hall and Jefferson 1975), the aim was to dismantle the idea of a unified 'youth culture' and explore how youth subcultures related to class cultures and the generation of cultural hegemony in post-war Britain. The definition of culture owes a great deal to the conception of a 'way of life' from Raymond Williams. For Hall and Jefferson (1975: 10–11), culture includes maps of meaning through which social experiences acquire intelligibility. They explored how the occupation of deviant and non-conformist subject positions often expressed working-class values. A succession of Teds, Mods, Rockers, Skinheads and Punks had not only rejected the constraints imposed by their parents but also were using style to parade their resistance to those who would have them behave in more acceptable ways. For the CCCS researchers, the stylistic improvisation of identities within youth cultures was a political act, rejecting middle class expectations, admittedly in economic conditions where high youth unemployment had made such expectations especially unrealistic.

This account drew heavily upon the sociological concepts of interactionist and ethnomethodological studies of crime and deviance considered in Chapter 2. Of note in these ethnographic studies was their account of the processes whereby people occupying authoritative decision-making positions were able to label and categorize individuals as belonging to particular group types. These types ranged from officially sanctioned labels such as 'juvenile delinquents' and 'persistent offenders' to casual and informal classificatory practices where certain groups were identified as (and lived up to the reputation of) 'trouble-makers' and 'problem children'. The representation of youth subcultures as folk devils and the generation of moral panics through media amplification of deviance had already been outlined in Stanley Cohen's (1972/1987) study of Mods and Rockers from which the CCCS were able to draw a rich vocabulary. The recognition of the role of press hysteria and the exaggeration of the threat from youth subcultures to the social fabric drew the sociological focus to media representations. The focus on the symbolic dimension also indicated their acceptance of Roland Barthes' (1973) account of semiology as part of the mix of ideas. The study of the forms of dress also led them to consider the connotations of teddy boy uniforms which had reversioned Edwardian suits from London's second-hand markets through bright colour and the use of satin and other embellishments parodied Edwardian dress codes in order to mimic the acquisition of status.

> Originally, the Edwardian suit was introduced in 1950 by a group of Savile Row tailors who were attempting to initiate a new style. It was addressed, primarily to the young aristocratic men about town . . . This dress began to be taken up by working class youths sometime in 1953 . . . Modifications to this style by the Teds were bootlace tie; thick-creped shoes (Eton clubman chukka type); skin tight, drain-pipe trousers (without turnups); straighter, less waisted jackets; moleskin or satin collars to the jackets; and the addition of vivid colours. The earlier sombre suit colours occasionally gave way to suits of vivid green, red or pink and other 'primitive' colours.
>
> (Jefferson 1975: 85)

The improvisation and the establishment of connections with greased back quiffed hair, rock and roll music and an attitude where excessive touchiness to insults was expected, all helped to establish a strong group identity. Dick Hebdige's (1975) study of the meanings attached to Mod identity also indicated a desire for status although here conspicuous material consumption was closely connected to the dance culture and the use of drugs like 'speed'. Similarly, traditional working-class clothes from the 1930s to the 1950s were subject to exaggerated imaginary treatment in the mix of T-shirts, braces, tight jeans and heavy 'Doc Marten's' boots unified through the close cropped 'suede head' hair cut which appropriated memories of the concentration camps to construct an image of disaffected otherness. This was an aggressive but largely a defensive response to the forced dislocation that occurred as part of urban resettlement from the slums of the inner cities in the 1950s and 1960s. Skinhead subcultures engineered a magical recovery of the lost sense of community. According to Jon Clarke (1975), the skinheads embodied a desperate desire to reclaim a sense of belonging and rootedness which fed into racist and homophobic language and violence. These were vibrant active and motivated responses to changing socio-economic conditions. As Hebdige neatly summarizes:

WORKING CLASS + MOD + SPEED = ACTION
MIDDLE CLASS + HIPPIE + MARIJUANA = PASSIVITY
(Hebdige 1975: 96)

Yet this desire to conform to a stereotypical imaginary community also had significant consequences in terms of sexual and racial attitudes. Indeed, these are studies of male subcultures where girls are marginalized or fit in with prevailing stereotypes. Angela McRobbie and Jenny Garber concluded that a comparable study of female youth culture, experiences and resistances would have to be conducted in very different social spaces (McRobbie and Garber 1975). A direct illustration of the androcentric fixation comes from the second key example of cultural research at the CCCS by one of the members of *Resistance through Rituals* team, Paul Willis.

In *Learning to Labour: How Working Class Kids Get Working Class Jobs* (1977) Willis uses the qualitative research method of in-depth interviews with 12 teenage boys to reconstruct their attitudes to each other, girls, cultural difference, education and their future working lives in 'Hammertown' (which was Wolverhampton, near Birmingham in the industrial West Midlands region of the UK). The boys in question derided boys who studied hard as 'earoles', conducted a war of attrition against their teachers in order to 'have a laff' and celebrated their own failure in academic attainment. They demonstrated (very explicitly) racist and sexist attitudes and embraced the prospect that on the day when they could leave school they could achieve a 'manly' manual job with the benefits it would bring. In previous sociological studies of education and youth, immediate gratification and present day orientation had been seen as a function of cultural deprivation and even educational subnormality. In this neo-Gramscian treatment of the educational processes and subjective identification these were the children of the working classes not just being schooled for fitting in with the capitalist social order (as factory fodder): they walked into it willingly. In this research, Willis (1977) was tangibly pinpointing the level at which the hegemonic struggle as a battle for the hearts and minds of the people had to be conducted.

Culture and political change

The research project which brought these concerns together in a coherent and political way was the CCCS study group on mugging. The resulting publication, *Policing the Crisis* (Hall *et al.* 1978) explored the specific consequences of the changing economic context and its affects on political culture. The fiscal crisis of the state in the 1970s combined with a long term decline in capitalist productivity since the mid-1960s resulted in a breakdown in the negotiated relationship between employers and unions, specifically the strategically important miners' unions. The result was greater industrial conflict and associated discord elsewhere. In an Althusserian moment, Hall *et al.* (1978) argued that since the ideological mechanisms which secured consent had now failed, then a more coercive approach would have to be adopted by the state to maintain the social and political order. If capitalist restructuring were to be achieved then this would require a shift in policing and the criminal justice system so that the side-effects of change could be managed. The operationalization of the repressive state apparatuses required some degree of active consent. The mugging study group argued that the generation of moral panics through the mass media over crime and mugging had resulted in the identification of ethnic minorities (alongside union shop stewards and radical activists) as the 'folk devils' responsible for moral and social decline and disorder. This had provided the ideological ammunition for the development of the 'law and order' agenda of the mid-1970s. The spiral of signification through which young black men had become the media scapegoat for social ills provided a setting in which right wing politics could use the race card as part of a hegemonic project on behalf of capitalist interests. The media and culture should be seen as the terrain on which the hegemonic struggle could be conducted. Hall *et al.* (1978) argued that if anyone could bottle the underlying fears of the British people and sell them as a political message they would change the face of British politics. This is exactly what happened; Thatcherite politics used the fears lurking beneath the surface of British culture in order to *disarticulate* the values and assumptions through which social democracy had largely dominated since the 1940s. In its place the Thatcherite project *rearticulated* them in such a way that collectivism could only be seen as an intrusion in private life, an expression of the 'nanny state', rather than as a 'benevolent patriarch' protecting the people from the cradle to the grave. In the process, unemployment, homelessness and poverty came to be redefined as personal troubles rather than social problems.

In *Policing the Crisis* we see the building blocks for characterizing Thatcherism as 'authoritarian populism' (Hall 1980, 1983a,

1983b). The neo-Gramscian account of the social transformations in the late 1970s and early 1980s is informed by two key positions. First, the identification of an emerging *authoritarian statism,* drawing from *State, Power, Socialism* (1978) by Nicos Poulantzas. Second, the Gramscian conceptions of *passive revolution* and *hegemony*, which had been used as a basis for conceptualizing populism by Ernesto Laclau (1977). Hall was most concerned that the left had dwelt too much upon the economic relations of capitalism to the detriment of their understanding of the struggles within the political and ideological superstructure. This became especially important as the political right managed to monopolize the popular-democratic field just as 'the question of democracy became the principal site of struggle' (Hall 1980: 158). Hall's account was actually a plea to the left to take democracy more seriously at a time when the political right were successfully articulating popular support against the social democratic power bloc (a passive revolution from below) around the theme of the defence of law and the social order in a complex war of position.

Since popular democratic discourses are constructed through the contradiction between the people and the power bloc, the treatment of the social democratic power bloc as statist, bureaucratic and as creeping collectivism becomes an easy contrast for the individual choice, freedom and personal responsibility of Thatcherite populist discourse. Indeed, Thatcherism did capture the moral high ground in the 1980s. However, when the Conservatives came to power in 1979 the populism shifted away from active mobilization of popular demands and served merely to secure active consent against opposition within the party system and the state. Hall described this as a populist ventriloquism which has accelerated the centralization of power within the state at the expense of parliamentary representation. In this way, the crisis is not portrayed as 'a mirror of politics' reflecting a given set of economic conditions but as a strategic terrain of struggle and contestation for the construction of popular consent for an increasingly authoritarian regime. Enough about politics for now, but what about its consequences for cultural studies.

The emergence of a buoyant consumer-driven market order did transform the cultural landscape in the UK and US and, with that, cultural studies during the 1980s; most significantly, by redirecting the attention of cultural studies away from production towards consumption and the uses of culture in everyday life. The political economy approaches of the 1970s lacked the conceptual vocabulary to fully deal with this shift and a variety of approaches loosely labelled as postmodern emerged in their place. These approaches focused on style, representation and cultural consumption, in order to provide what amounts to a descriptive outline of some of the major changes of our time such as the emergence of the information society and globalization. This study has separated postmodern from post-structuralist approaches in order to emphasize the importance of the latter for social scientific practice. Postmodern approaches provided a very lively refiguring of the substantive focus of inquiry in social research in the 1980s, especially problematizing essences and foundations in a variety of fields. However, little in the way of a conceptual legacy has emerged other than that established by post-structuralist theory. Hence, I am deliberately marginalizing post-modernism in this narrative (see Lyon 1994). (For a more detailed discussion of postmodernism and scientific knowledge, specifically on Lyotard's rearticulation of Wittgenstein's concept of language games, see Smith 1998b: ch. 7.)

In working through the practical problems of deploying the Marxist framework in a rapidly changing and complex cultural context, many members of the CCCS were led to rethink the logic of mediation and their concern for emphasizing the underlying primacy of political economy. Plainly, the careful analysis of these shifts in political culture and the changing concerns of cultural studies, so that class analysis could also find a way of accommo-dating gender and ethnicity, demanded a more flexible and ade-quate way of explaining the production of meaning. The looser neo-Gramscian formulation whereby no guarantees existed that the economy shapes culture offered one way out. Also significant was the characterization of the articulation and rearticulation of cultural elements as involving constant struggles for dominance and the generation of resistance without assuming that they have their roots in class interests (Laclau and Mouffe 1985). The concern shifted to the political and ideological struggle for hegemony and establishing the longer term reconstruction of an alternative hegemonic common sense. However, the metaphors of struggle, social antagonism and conflict remain.

Towards culture as a contested space

Social identities are therefore accomplished through struggle; they are fluid and open to continual transformation and they are never

complete but unfinished business. Stuart Hall and others at the
CCCS challenged the idea that cultural representation should be
read as a simple manifestation of some class interest. They regarded
communication and cultural interpretation as an arena for the
negotiation of meanings and defined popular culture in a relational
way. In particular, this approach recognizes that the definition of
cultural categories varies with changing social relations. Instead of
defining popular culture as an inferior culture, the CCCS argued
that its meaning depends upon its relationship with other categories. In short, since the meaning of the 'popular' can only be
understood by how it relates to categories such as high, elite and
minority culture, we must acknowledge that these are constantly on
the move. Defining culture in this way is a distinct break from the
way in which objects are defined in social science as a discrete thing
which exists, for the purpose of inquiry as separate from the
inquirer.

As research was conducted and accumulated in the areas identified earlier by Hoggart and Williams – especially on the cultures of
class, youth, education, and region – then it became more apparent
that the idea that culture was simply an expression of some underlying set of conditions no longer made sense. The uses of neo-
Gramscian analysis of hegemony in the study of culture focused
attention upon the ways in which social forces are engaged in a constant struggle for political, intellectual and moral leadership. In the
work of Hall and his collaborators, we can see a useful example of
how culture could be redefined. The logic of mediation assumes
that culture is a manifestation of some underlying foundation. Of
course, as a Marxist, Gramsci had been concerned primarily with
class forces as well as with other categories such as intellectuals.
Hall and other CCCS participants recognized that other forms of
social antagonism operated alongside class (specifically, differences
in sexuality, gender, ethnicity and age). This meant that cultural
contestation had to be understood as a much looser process than
previously assumed by Marxists who adopted an approach to
culture based upon the logic of mediation. Marxists had believed
that it was possible to identify an example of cultural representation, say surrealist poetry, and trace its 'origins' back to some class
interest as a fixed point of reference, in this example as an expression of the petit bourgeois class (small shopkeepers). Even Bourdieu had tied taste distinctions to the maintenance of hierarchies
founded upon social class differences. The logic of articulation, on

the other hand, assumes that there are no necessary links between class and culture. In this way, cultural representation is seen constantly open to challenge (that the elements can be disarticulated and rearticulated) rather than determined by an underlying structure.

By approaching culture through the use of the idea of hegemony, culture can be conceptualized as a space within which struggles between social forces are conducted. As with many who emerged from the Marxist tradition (not least the nameless postmodernists) Hall challenged the idea that one should read cultural representation as a manifestation of some class interest. He regarded communication and cultural interpretation as an arena for the negotiation of meanings and defined popular culture in a relational way. Like the semiologists, discussed earlier, Hall asks us to recognize that definition of cultural categories varies with the changing relations in the cultural field. Instead of defining popular culture as an inferior culture, he argues that its meaning depends upon its relationship with other categories, that is, the meaning of the popular can only be understood by how it related to categories such as high, elite and minority culture.

> From period to period, the contents of each category changes. Popular forms become enhanced in cultural value, go up the cultural escalator – and find themselves on the opposite side. Other things cease to have high cultural value, and are appropriated into the popular, becoming transformed in the process. The structuring principle does not consist of the contents of each category – which, I insist, will alter from one period to another. Rather it consists of the forces and relations which sustain the distinction, the difference: roughly, between what, at any time, counts as an elite culture activity or form, and what does not.
>
> (Hall 1981: 234)

To summarize, Hall draws upon a range of approaches; we will focus on two of these in order to highlight the idea of the articulation of meaning. Marxism does provide an analysis of the social in terms of struggle and contestation. However, the treatment of cultural forms as an ideological expression of underlying economic interests simply proved unsatisfactory. One consequence has been the increased concern with issues surrounding consumption rather than production within cultural studies itself (see Miller 1995). The analysis of hegemony, that is, the way in which social forces are engaged in a constant struggle for political, intellectual and moral

(if you prefer, cultural) leadership is also especially important.
More important still is how we define a social force. Unlike Gramsci, we don't have to be so confined to classes, fractions and a
limited range of social categories for many other forms of social
antagonism are relevant. In this way we can become concerned with
identity formation in a variety of social and political movements
engaged in complex articulatory practices (only some of which may
happen to be based on some construction of social class). This
means that cultural contestation can be understood as a looser
process than that assumed by those who have adopted an approach
to culture based upon the logic of mediation. The idea of identifying a cultural text, artefact or practice and tracing its 'origins' back
to some fixed point of reference seems especially inappropriate,
simplistic and misleading. In the next chapter we consider the implications of the logic of articulation in more detail.

5

Contested Cultural Spaces: Identity, Discourse and the Body

So far, we have established that culture involves the lived intersubjective symbolic relationships through which we understand the conditions in which we live. Indeed, each of the ways in which we explored the idea of culture so far (and how it has been classified) are situated. They are part and parcel of systems of representation which regulate the production of meaning. In short, these theories are distinctive attempts to make sense of who we are and in what kind of social relations we exist. They also define what we can and can not take seriously. Culture is at once a product of fragile connections established between the various elements of language and it is also bound by the institutions which are themselves the product of cultural practices. If culture is a linguistic, symbolic and dialogic set of relations, it is also contingent and its elements can be disarticulated and rearticulated. This directly challenges the structuralist accounts of language considered earlier and breaks with the belief that the visible manifestations of language are determined by an underlying total structure. Rather than seeing meaningful communication as a momentary expression of a fixed language system, the construction of meaning involves the transformation of floating elements into temporarily fixed moments (Laclau and Mouffe 1985: 93–148; Laclau 1990: 3–85).

If communication and cultural interpretation involve the negotiation of meanings and are seen as characteristically contested, this is a distinct break from the way in which objects of analysis have been conventionally defined in social science. But it is not only culture and related areas of social science which have been reassessed in this way. The objects of analysis in a variety of different fields of knowledge have been subject to the same can-opener, prising out their imaginary figures and laying bare their foundations as convenient fictions. Even studies of medical science, especially in the field of the history of medical practice (Porter 1987), have begun to question the taken-for-granted assumptions about the character of the human *body* and its relationship to the *mind*. Indeed, recent approaches would argue that the retention of the mind/body distinction is itself part of the problem. Turner (1995) argues that both of these categories are discursively constituted and ought to be seen as situated within institutional practices devoted to the regulation of bodies in the interests of the professional organizations.

> To regard illness as a text open to a variety of perspectives is a radical approach to sickness, because it points to some of the problems in the medical model which underlies the basis of institutionalized, scientific technologically directed medicine ... Modern medicine, treating the body as a sort of machine, regards illness and disease as malfunctions of the body's mechanics. All 'real' diseases have specific causal mechanisms which can be ultimately identified and treated. Such an approach rules out the centrality and importance of experience, feeling, emotion and interpretation in the phenomenology of sickness and disease.
>
> (Turner 1995: 205–6)

In this way Turner (1995) seeks to find a way of theorizing the embodied self and its relationship to these kinds of regulative practices. Later, we shall focus on illustrations on the role of 'the body' in recent social scientific practice. This treatment of culture (or for that matter, the body) as a contested space or terrain fits particularly well with the post-structuralist understanding of discourse as an ongoing play of meaning without origin or end. It is the implications of post-structuralism for understanding identity that we now turn.

Rethinking identity through the text

The idea that our identities are both well defined and clearly visible has been under attack throughout the twentieth century. The concept of the self as always in process and under construction has been a feature of sociological approaches such as interactionism (see Chapter 2). Similarly, the recognition that the self was fragmented and beset by contradictions (achieving a temporary unity through myths and the process of interpellation) has featured in structuralist approaches to culture. Nevertheless, there was always an attempt to ground the self in some firm reality, such as experience or underlying social structure. Post-structuralism, however, starts from the premise that all such groundings and foundations are linguistic constructs and that these constructs are organized in symbolic systems through which the world comes to have the appearance of solidity. The history of social science is littered with attempts to claim that the knowledge produced is authoritative, serving as a fixed point of reference. This critical reassessment focused our attention on the architects of 'truth', the academics who devised the procedures and criteria for accepting a particular account of 'reality as authentic and authoritative'.

In Chapter 4, you were introduced to the early writings of Roland Barthes and his development of Saussure's account of language as a relational system into one that could aid our understanding of the emergence of mythologies. Barthes suggested that signs can become empty signifiers which can carry parasitic messages. Here we focus on how the semiological approach to language and culture unfolded in his writings. The claim that we were witnessing the death of the 'author' is as much an attempt to persuade us to reassess the way we trust the author's voice (as an expression of the writer's intentions) as it is to challenge the assumptions of literary criticism. The upshot was to highlight the complexity of the inter-relationship between readers and writers as the site where meanings were produced. His work therefore embodies a struggle with the problems of structuralist assumptions, one which finally led him to unravel them. Of note is the way that Barthes problematized the distinction between denotation and connotation by suggesting that all descriptive words or statements connote meaning.

It is useful to take an example from his studies in literary criticism. In *S/Z* (1970), an exploration of Balzac's *Sarrasine* (an example of the realist genre which represented early nineteenth century France), Barthes demonstrates how the references to reality are no more than rearticulations of previous writings. Barthes meticulously broke down the elements of *Sarrasine* and identified how Balzac had engaged in an appropriation of commonly expressed sentiments on morals, psychology, aesthetics and history in a particular time and place (often through the use of crude stereotypes). To do this, Barthes identified five codes at work in the text. The *hermeneutic code* introduces, defines and resolves the enigma (the underlying mystery) within the narrative (such as 'who or what is *Sarrasine*?). The *proairetic code* is concerned with the development of the narrative; it lays out the stages or actions through which the story moves (Barthes identified 561 lexies in the sequence within *Sarrasine*). Together these codes regulate the sequence in the story, propelling the reader forwards. The *symbolic code* involves the oppositions upon which the narrative rests such as good/bad, life/death, masculine/feminine, interior/exterior and so on. The *semic code* (or code of signifiers) involves the hints of meaning attached to the word or sentences, such as the use of tenses (indicating the femininity of Sarrasine) or possibly the moral assumptions involved in the use of a particular expression. Together these organize the meanings of situations, events and characters. The *referential (or cultural) code* organizes the references to the reality beyond the text. It involves the phrases and terms which imply a common stock of knowledge held by writers and readers so that the words used appear to be unproblematic descriptions (Barthes 1970; Eco 1984). In short, the connections between signifiers and signified are produced by the activity of reading itself, and do not exist prior to this, transforming the way in which texts are understood. He concluded that 'the birth of the reader must be at the cost of the death of the Author' (Barthes 1977: 148).

This analysis of textual complexity draws upon a distinction which is very relevant to the construction of social scientific knowledge. Barthes distinguishes between works and texts. 'Works' are *lisible* (readerly), they are authoritative accounts which cannot be rewritten by the audience. Their characteristic journey is linear, moving in one direction from a beginning to a preordained end. 'Texts', however, are *scriptible* (writerly), for their form enables readers to rewrite and appropriate the text as they read them. Moreover, he argues the relationship between a text and a reader is a qualitatively different one. The reader's response is more intimate and full of enjoyment (*jouissance*), for it problematizes our assumptions and values, disconcerting our sense of the order of things.

> Text of pleasure: the text that contents, fills, grants euphoria; the text
> that comes from culture and does not break with it, is linked to a com-
> fortable practice of reading. Text of bliss: the text that imposes a sense

of loss, the text that discomforts (perhaps to the point of a certain boredom), unsettles the reader's historical, cultural, psychological assumptions, the consistency of his tastes, values, memories, brings to a crisis his relation with language.

(Barthes 1976: 14)

Our response to the *lisible* text involves pleasure (*plaisir*) but it is the comforting kind which is produced by getting what we expect; it fulfils our expectations and confirms our prejudices. This is the dull satisfaction of hearing again that the world is as it should. It secures our compliance, for we feel unable to question or interrupt the author's voice. Of course, as Barthes' own example demonstrates, this hard distinction between a work and a text is more of an ideal type (a simplistic exaggeration) than an accurate description (certainly it runs against the current all-inclusive use of the word, text). *Sarrasine* is encoded in ways that attempt to close down the readers' opportunities for rewriting meanings yet this can never be completely accomplished. Readers may find that it is uncomfortable to read against the grain but they will still have opportunities to destabilize and subvert the encoded messages. Indeed, the classificatory practices of literary criticism can make the effort of challenging the received approach very difficult. Nonetheless, there is always scriptibility in any lisible project or, put another way, all readerly works contain a writerly text waiting to get out. At the end of the day, readerly accounts of the world only work when the members of the audience have been socialized into acquiescence, to the point that such writing tells them what they expect to hear and the assumptions involved are taken for granted.

Our role here is to explore how this approach can help us change the conduct of recent social scientific practice (creating the context in which the figure of the social scientist as aloof and detached expert can be placed in question). The history of social science is that of a succession of authoritative texts, each demonstrating many of the characteristics identified by the concept of the 'work'. The encoded messages are more deeply ingrained and social scientific audiences have, on the whole, been more carefully and systematically socialized into the procedures of their respective fields of inquiry than literary audiences. In addition, models of learning within the social sciences have often taken the view that education is a transmission device for maintaining an academic tradition. Writings can be read in different ways and the reader is a 'proactive' agent who can participate in the production of meaning, establishing their own connections, building their own stories, rewriting the narrative. This means that, rather than considering the products of social scientific research as reflections of the 'real world', we should redirect our attention to the relationship between the writers and audiences of social science. We shall return to an example of what it means to 'rewrite' social scientific works in Chapter 6.

Similarly, when we look at other post-structuralist interventions, we can also find approaches that can help us understand social scientific knowledge. Working at the interface of philosophy, history and literature, Jacques Derrida claimed that many key concepts are conjuring tricks for pretending that problems do not exist (using a name such as being, truth or objectivity to cover them up). Drawing upon Heideggerian phenomenology, Derrida placed such words 'under erasure', indicating their ambiguous status as inadequate but, in the absence of a something better, it remains quite necessary. In particular, he argued that the concept of 'the subject' should be placed under erasure in the same way. Using this critical technique, Derridean discourse analysis destabilizes the key ideas upon which western knowledge is grounded; i.e. in logocentrism. Rather than searching for some underlying foundation or essence, this approach suggests that we should map the conceptual landscape for the metaphoric and metonymic relations which provide a sense of order.

To do this, we have to engage in the interrogation of texts to establish their organization around certain oppositional categories; such as true/false, rationality/irrationality, objective/subjective, masculine/femininity and same/other (Derrida 1973, 1976, 1978). One side of the opposition is positively valued and placed in a privileged position, that is the dominant one. This approach has served well in the study of cultural differences where the distinction between same/other features heavily. By carefully mapping the relations of equivalence (of sameness) and difference (of otherness) we can identify the ways in which cultural differences are constructed around the ideas of insiders and outsiders and how they can be articulated with other oppositions, like rationality/irrationality, civilized/primitive, instrumental/expressive and so on. For example, Edward Said (1978) argued that despite the variety of ways of thinking about the Orient (in history, literature, comic books and television programmes) 'the westerner' has always been placed in a position of superiority. This is a product of a long complicated history of symbolic representations and associations in European culture but has served as an organizing device for the classificatory practices in knowledge construction.

> The scientist, the scholar, the missionary, the trader, or the soldier was in or thought about, the Orient because he could be there, or could think about it, with very little resistance on the Orient's part. Under the general heading of knowledge of the Orient, and within the umbrella of Western hegemony over the Orient during the period from the end of the eighteenth century, there emerged a complex Orient suitable for study in the academy, for display in the museum, for reconstruction in the colonial office, for theoretical illustration in anthropological, biological, linguistic, racial and historical theses about mankind and the universe, for instances of economic and socio-logical theories of development, revolution, cultural personality, national or religious character. Additionally, the imaginary examin-ation of things Oriental was based on more or less exclusively upon a Western consciousness out of whose unchallenged centrality an Ori-ental world emerged, first according to general ideas about who and what was an Oriental, then according to a detailed logic governed not simply by empirical reality but by a battery of desires, repressions, investments, and projections.
>
> (Said 1978: 6)

There is a great deal more informing Said's position than the Der-ridean concern to lay bare the opposition of same/other but this brief extract provides a powerful illustration of how oppositional relationships matter in the way we understand the world. Moreover the unifying elements in European identity have only been forged through the articulation of a series of imaginary Orients, many of them sexualized through male fantasies of the feminized represen-tations involved. These were rearticulated in more complex ways following the discovery of the New World (Hall 1992). In short, identities come to attain a unity and purpose through the operation of the same/other relation; that we are who we are because we are able to invent and reinvent how we are different from others. Con-temporary accounts of cultural difference have emerged as a prod-uct of Saussure's conception of the production of meaning through relations of difference. This reinterpretation of Saussure's approach to language leads us to think about the relationship between signifiers and signifieds in new ways.

Like Saussure, Derrida not only identifies meaning as relational but he also assumes that any attempt to fix the meaning of a sign is doomed to fail for there is always a surplus meaning, a 'supplement' which leaves the meaning of a sign open to disarticulation and rearticulation. According to Derrida, Saussure was engaged in the privileging of speech (direct and unmediated form of communi-cation) over writing (portrayed as an oblique re-representation). This characterization of writing as an imperfect disguise for lan-guage can better be seen as a device to consign to writing all the features of language that Saussure did not wish to accommodate in his approach. So the legacy is twofold and contradictory: Saussure continues the tradition in which the 'metaphysics of presence' pre-vails; yet he provides a conceptualization of language as relational which deprivileges all words as foundations (for there are no posi-tive terms only differences).

Part of the confusion in interpreting Derrida's arguments stems from the difficulties of translation. Difference has a double meaning; there are relations of difference through which meanings are produced (*différence*) as well as the sense of difference as deferred that no meaning 'is ever finished' and always in process (*différance*). Meaning is always unstable and provisional (Derrida 1978, 1981). Just as it is no longer possible to permanently fix the meaning of cultural identities, it is also no longer possible to think in terms of a single unified text. Each text exists by virtue of its relations with other texts; the condition of intertextuality. The meanings produced constantly change and there is no original source of meaning, only a flow of signifiers which can be disarticu-lated from existing texts and rearticulated in different combinations in the construction of new texts.

Discourse analysis is particularly useful as a technique for explor-ing the role of identities and representations in the organization of social life but, more than that, it also highlights the way in which these identities and representations are constantly open to change, that they are always unfinished business. Stability is provided by the classificatory practices through which texts are catalogued and given a value. Certain texts or for that matter literary styles through their careful reproduction and use by the custodians of the literary traditions in the academy and other sites of authoritative commen-tary can attain the status of a canon. These serve as the reference points for making sense of and valuing new texts. Intertextuality also acknowledges the production of meaning by readers, although we should also remember that all writers are readers first.

In effect, the writings of Barthes and Derrida helped to shift the

ground of debate away from an overwhelming concern with meanings as bound by the text. This contributed towards the realization
that audience reception is as important, if not more so, as encoded
messages. But audiences do not exist in a vacuum; they have an
investment in a variety of knowledges and they produce meaning
in a wide range of institutional practices. To understand how the
production of meaning is organized and regulated we need to turn
to Foucault's genealogical approach. Next, we address the ways in
which this approach to culture has led to considerable attention to
the cultural meanings of the body. The exploration of the body as
a 'contested space' owes much to the above approaches. However,
particular attention will be devoted to the idea of the 'body' as a
metaphor of cultural contradictions and social antagonisms and
how this has affected the way in which social research has constructed and understood social problems.

The body and power

The conceptual landscape of the social sciences has been radically
altered by the writings of Michel Foucault. Much like the previous
approaches, Foucault was concerned with representational complexity and the questions of how knowledge is produced within a
shared cultural context within definite historical circumstances. In
his early structuralist writings he explored the question of how it
was possible to establish 'truth' when the concept had its own history with many meanings? To understand the varied uses of the category of truth, he argued that we had to look at the discourse of
which it was a part, the system of representation which regulates
what meanings can or cannot be produced. Discourses, he went to
argue, involve configurations of rules of conduct, established texts
and institutional practices each situated in a historically and socially
specific set of cultural relations. In this way, we can see that he was
mainly concerned with the relationship between knowledge and
power relations (Foucault 1970, 1972, 1980, 1982). The power/
knowledge relationship is illustrated throughout his work. In the
writings on madness, punishment and sexuality, he explores how
the way we think about normality and pathology, the modes of
classification through which people are pigeon-holed. In addition,
he exposes the role of truth claims in giving credence to the culturally specific judgements of experts and how they have had concrete
effects on people's lives.

The human and social sciences have often treated human beings as objects to be studied in a dispassionate and detached way and placed within a scientific classification system. In this way, the human beings so classified have been objectified and dehumanized in the name of human progress. For example, in developmental psychopathology we can see how the identification of particular 'conditions' often draws upon commonly held cultural presumptions about normal and abnormal behaviour. Academic descriptions of children labelled as autistic as 'odd outsiders' or those labelled schizophrenic as 'bizarre' is compounded by the more standard use of terminology which carries derogatory connotations, such as 'retarded', 'disorder', 'flawed', 'abnormal' and 'disturbed'. Each word carries with it the prospect of pathologization. The whole field of psychopathology and a substantive part of psychology are engaged in the classification of people into types. Rather than recognizing that such types are constructions, there is the constant danger that the classificatory practices are seen as a mirror reflection of the way the world is organized. So far, we have focused on the labelling or 'hailing' of people rather than the reasons why we invest so much in subject positions. The acquisition of a psychopathological subject position can itself offer a form of haven for it offers the reassurance of support (that someone cares enough to categorize me) to the person so classified or the parents of the children mentioned earlier. Many disabled people have labels thrust upon them whether they like it or not. This is in part a consequence of the labels applied by medical practitioners which can serve to set them apart from others. Such labels can be both:

- enabling by releasing resources (such as additional nursing support in the home or with the provision of special educational needs) or generate recognition that needs must be met
- constraining by limiting the potential of disabled people to develop an individual's talents fully, perhaps because an employer does not believe a disabled person can cope with additional responsibilities.

Much of the difficulty stems from the role of the medical model, which defined disability as a medical problem. This approach assumed that 'the disabled' could be defined through conventional medical classification systems and treated accordingly in the 'right conditions'. It was also assumed that a particular 'condition' could be 'treated' in the same way regardless of the specific needs of the person in question. Being visibly disabled was seen as an obstacle to 'the patient's' progress and they were expected to 'fit in' to 'normal life' through the use of, for example, prosthetic limbs to conceal their disability. This was part of a wider set of practices and beliefs about appropriate health care (such as the Truby King method of childrearing, which included 'feeding by the clock' where the routines of child care were subject to strict regimentation). Medical doctors were often treated as the source of authoritative knowledge on such matters and their instructions were often followed without question. It was not uncommon for those people with the severest disabilities to receive the least care and support on the grounds that they could not be made normal. For disabled people, this often meant that specific individual needs went unaddressed and they often had little or no control over their life choices. Supporters of the social model which emerged in the 1960s argued that the problems faced by disabled people were not caused by their impairments but by the beliefs, attitudes and practices of 'the non-disabled'; that it was society that had the problem and not the disabled people.

Pathologization and social exclusion tend to work together or, even worse, intensify one another. The medical definition of disability helped to ensure that disabled people were not only undervalued but also excluded from many of the practices of everyday life. In addition, the medical model had contributed to the social construction that disabled people are abnormal, threatening and even dangerous (to themselves and others). This discourse legitimized prejudice, discrimination and neglect in all aspects of social life. The disability movement has been instrumental in challenging the normalization and pathologization tendencies of medical and psychiatric practitioners, successfully disarticulating the assumptions and concepts which disparaged disabled people and rearticulating them in more positive ways. More recently, disability discourses have experienced some interesting interventions from the advocates of genetic or surgical intervention in order to prevent as well as remedy some forms of disability, potentially dividing the disability movement. For instance, cochlea implants offer the possibility of 'curing' some of the causes of deafness but this would also have a big impact on the future of the sign language community. New medical techniques for screening during pregnancy are also likely to mean that parents will be offered more information on the potential risks of giving birth to a disabled child. Consequently,

questions as to what is an acceptable and unacceptable disability
have been raised.

Since medical opinion is no longer seen as the sole source of
authoritative knowledge there has been considerable resistance to
emergent bioethical discourses. This has coincided with a shift in
welfare discourses where citizenship is increasingly tied up with
being seen to be playing a useful role in society. In the UK, this has
produced a series of measures which attempt to narrow the definition of disability in order to restructure benefit support (osten-
sibly to 'target the most needy'). The way that we define disability
has now been rearticulated with assumptions about a disabled
person's physical capacity to participate in the workforce. The
social model's insistence on participating in everyday life has been
hijacked in the New Labour march towards social efficiency. If I can
present a disturbing future scenario drawing these discursive shifts
together: how long before disabled individuals lose financial
support by rejecting medical intervention or parents face the full
cost of looking after disabled children they decided to keep rather
than abort? Foucault's insight that the more we intervene (in the
name of humanitarianism) the more harm we do is especially
relevant here (see Foucault 1967, 1973). Disability discourses
operate as systems of representation constituted by evolving rules
of conduct which (through reference to the established corpus of
knowledge embodied in established texts) which regulate what
meanings can and cannot be produced in institutional practices.
They make a difference to people's lives. What matters, of course,
is the kind of difference they make.

In choosing an example such as disability I wanted to steer clear
of the usual illustrations of Foucault's approach drawing from criminology. The operation of power and resistance is constantly played
out within a variety of institutional contexts, not always as bleak as
the prison and the asylum (the sociological favourites when discussing Foucault). The genealogical approach identified the complex
techniques which regulate, control and keep people under surveillance. It also addresses the role played by the academy in providing
the terms of reference and the legitimacy for such processes,
whereby social scientists impose their own culturally specific presumptions and prejudices on the object of analysis with which they
were concerned. In the processes of objectification we can also see
how social scientific knowledge is involved in a complex process of
constructing the identities of those they seek to study. Knowledge

creates new 'subjects' and identifies what is normal and abnormal in relationship to them. The social agents of knowledge (the scientists, doctors, teachers, social workers, police officers, social security officers – in short, anyone with the institutional power to define the identity of anyone else) are involved in activities which reinforce the powerlessness of the marginalized and excluded in the social order.

One of the weaknesses of the approaches which had drawn upon linguistics was the neglect of history and the mechanisms through which discourses, as systems of representation, are open to change and transformation. Foucault suggested that these changes take place through the institutional practices in which discourses regulated the production of meaning. So, in Foucault's account we can see how discourses are transformed and reorganized by tracing the operation of the distinctions such as the normal and the pathological. By assessing people against distinctions such as rational/irrational, normal/abnormal and so on, social scientists are also moral agents. They judge behaviour against cultural values and, in turn, these values only make sense within the discourses concerned. The 'subject position' is discursively constituted in two different ways. Discourses produce subjects, which are the imaginary figures who personify the forms of knowledge in specific social and historical locations. These figures have the attributes expected in the stereotype of, for example, 'the dangerous queer' or 'the rational criminal'. The subject is often reinvented through a succession of closely connected figures such as 'delinquent youth', 'problem families', the 'emotionally disturbed child' or, to pick out an example from earlier, the 'black mugger' (Hall *et al.* 1978) and so on. The discourse also regulates the production of meaning by reference to these kinds of figures, situating the reader/viewer. In this way, the discourse operates as a frame of reference through which particular kinds of established knowledge make sense and through which we become the bearers of its power/knowledge (Hall 1997: 56).

Social scientists invent and reinvent 'new subject positions' in a way that allows social researchers to identify the normality and abnormality and the rationality and irrationality of human behaviour. This is more than a revamped labelling theory of deviance. Discourses offer incentives for all the participants to invest in the subject positions articulated within them. We are often translated from active into docile bodies quite willingly. How is this achieved? The same practices of surveillance (combined with the careful and appropriate use of punishment), and even the organization of space, which Foucault identifies in the criminal justice system can be seen in the institutional practices with which social scientists are concerned (in schools, the council estate, the casualty department, the shopping mall or on the football terraces). These 'disciplinary technologies' or 'panoptic' practices are part of all aspects of the institutional life of modern societies.

> The carceral texture of society assures both the real capture of the body and its perpetual observation; it is, by its very nature, the apparatus of punishment that conforms most completely to the new economy of power and the instrument of the formation of knowledge that this economy needs. Its panoptic functioning enables it to play this double role. By virtue of its methods of fixing, dividing, recording, it has been one of the simplest . . . most indispensable conditions for the development of this immense activity of examination that has objectified human behaviour . . . I am not saying that the human sciences emerged from the prison . . . it is because they have been conveyed by a specific and new modality of power . . . a certain way of rendering the group of men docile and useful. This policy required the involvement of definite relations of knowledge in relations of power; it called for the technique of overlapping subjection and objectification; it brought with it new procedures of individualization. The carceral network constituted one of the armatures of this power-knowledge that has made the human sciences historically possible. Knowable man, (soul, individuality, consciousness, conduct, whatever it is called) is the object effect of this analytical investment, of this domination-observation.
>
> (Foucault 1977: 304–5)

If we consider welfare institutions, we see how this can be applied. In *The Policing of Families* (1979), Jacques Donzelot argued that social services and welfare departments justify their own existence by reference to the need constantly to monitor personal relationships within families. From this perspective, much of post-war social science on the welfare state, poverty and social work, as well as specific knowledges on the 'deficiencies of families', are all implicated in the policing of personal life. Yet, historical accounts tend to celebrate the welfare state as the end product of a civilizing process, one which transforms the intrusions and interference in everyday life into a positive virtue. Although these conclusions are disturbing, they have still been described as the 'best account of the dark side of the social sciences' (Rorty 1994: 58) for demonstrating how scientific knowledge ensures that the excluded are also relatively powerless. However, discourses only work as systems of domination through the rules of conduct, texts and institutional practices where meaning is produced and the operation of power generates its own forms of resistance and subversion.

Discourses shape and become institutionalized in social policies and the organizations through which they are implemented. This also means that we need to pay attention to the informal arrangements and tacit assumptions that help the institutional practices adapt. They also produce the 'norms' against which deviation or abnormality is marked. If we look at Jon Clarke and Allan Cochrane's consideration of the institutionalization of discourses in relation to poverty we can see how state institutions and agencies monitor and intervene to encourage individuals to invest in particular kinds of subject positions (such as the 'deserving poor').

- *Poor people have to prove they are poor.* The systems of doing something about poverty . . . have always involved various sorts of tests that poor people have to pass to prove their need. . .There have also been morality tests – mainly directed at women – which examine whether they have been cohabiting . . .
- *Poor people must present themselves as poor.* They are claimants – an inferior and dependent social status, asking for something from society . . . subjects of the discourse [of poverty]
- *Poor people have things* done to *them.* Being poor is to be placed in a position where other people have rights over you. Society's institutional arrangements have sometimes been focused on *segregating* the poor – putting them in workhouses, for instance – to keep them away from the rest of 'us'. Sometimes they have been concerned to *normalize* the poor – giving lessons in budgetary management, good housekeeping, or parenting – with the aim of making 'them' more like 'us'. At other times the emphasis has been on maintaining surveillance on the poor – monitoring their behaviour to ensure they behave 'properly'.

(Clarke and Cochrane 1998: 35–6)

This is part of the 'trouble with normal' which besets social scientific investigations into poverty, crime, unemployment, mental illness and other 'social problems' – the moment we embark on a discussion of 'social problems' we are already navigating our way through the opposition between the normal and the pathological (Clarke 1998). This analysis of discourse in definite institutional sites within specific social and historical locations goes much further than Barthes and Derrida in offering a basis for concrete investigations. Foucault's writings on the body have also had an impact on

medical sociology (see Turner 1995) as well as on sexuality and the
self (Weeks 1985, 1989; McNay 1992, 1994). Turner (1995) argues
that the body has been subject to rationalization and standardization over a long period of time initially through medical clinics and
in the past hundred or so years this has been augmented by a range
of institutions for managing populations and drawing connections
between mental, physical and moral health (or sickness). The role
of eugenics and 'purity politics' in the emergence of family planning
indicate that the female body has always been a battleground. More
importantly, the medico-political discourses that have emerged
have been grounded in certain assumptions about normality. The
trouble with normal is that the only way it can be defined is by
identifying specific behaviours or characteristics as pathological.
The concern with the effects of regulation is especially evident in
the shifting discourses associated with sexual identity, as identified
in Jeffrey Weeks' historical narrative of the (re-)invention of the
figure of 'the homosexual'.

> The regulation of extra-marital sex has been a major concern for the
> forces of moral order throughout the history of the West, whether
> through the canonical controls of the church over adultery and
> sodomy in the medieval period, or the state's ordering of prostitution
> and homosexuality in the modern. Of all the 'variations' of sexual
> behaviour, homosexuality has had the most vivid social pressure, and
> has evoked the most lively (if usually grossly misleading) historical
> accounts . . . It has also, as an inevitable effect of the hostility it has
> evoked, produced the most substantial forms of resistance to hostile
> categorisation and has, consequently, a long cultural and subcultural
> history . . . Attitudes towards homosexual behaviour are, that is to say,
> culturally specific and have varied enormously across different cul-
> tures and through various historical periods . . . The physical acts
> might be similar, but their social implications are often profoundly
> different . . . The latter part of the nineteenth century, however, saw
> the clear emergence of new conceptualisations of homosexuality
> although the elements of the new definitions and practices can be
> traced to earlier periods. The sodomite, as Foucault has put it, was a
> temporary aberration. The 'homosexual', on the other hand, belonged
> to a species, and it is this new concern with the homosexual person,
> both in legal practice and in psychological and medical categorisation,
> that marks the crucial change, both because it provided a new subject
> of social observation and speculation, and because it opened up the
> possibility of new modes of self-articulation.
>
> (Weeks 1989: 96–102)

The history of (homo-)sexuality is thus a history of imaginary figures which can be reappropriated and rearticulated with positive messages. The emergence of gay identities which have to a greater or lesser extent been normalized in popular culture points to a weakness in dwelling too much on pathologization. There is a tendency in much Foucauldian literature to assume that the body is passive or an effect of regulatory practices, neglecting the role of resistance. Turner (1995) argues that phenomenology provides a way of filling this gap by directing our attention to the perspective of the patients and the taken for granted knowledge of everyday life.

When we look at how Foucault's approach has been articulated, some of the most useful applications have been synthesized with ideas from writers such as Derrida, Gilroy and Hall. In Anna Marie Smith's (1994) study, the construction of an identity involves the creation of a boundary which only makes sense when we consider the relations between the inside and the outside of that identity. Gilroy's exploration of the invention of the imaginary figure of the 'good black entrepreneur' as the 'citizen next door' in conservative politics is redeployed by Smith to explore the emergence of the 'good homosexual/dangerous queer' distinction in the moral panics around AIDS and Section 28 (a legislative measure which banned the 'intentional promotion of homosexuality' by local government in response to moral panics articulated in the 1980s). She reconstructs the complex ways in which gay male sexual identities are rearticulated through the use of the metaphors of 'invaders' and 'seducers'. Thus, Smith (1994) highlights the ways in which the meanings of racist and heterosexist discourses are intimately connected to the cultural assumptions and power relations of British society. Racist and homophobic representations in cultural politics in Britain were a vital component in the broader forms of political mobilization involved in Thatcherism in the 1970s and 1980s.

Why was this expression of anxiety around homosexuality, in this particular form, at this particular juncture, so persuasive? Why did the conception of the erosion of the social order through the promotion of homosexuality seem to 'sum up' otherwise disparate concerns, concerns about disease, morality, children and the family ... In the late 1980s, discourse on homosexuality was thoroughly intertwined with discourse on AIDS ... The search for the origin of AIDS is in turn nothing more than an attempt to ground this denial of the risks to heterosexuals; claims about the African and homosexual origins of

AIDS are shaped more by racist and anti-gay fantasies than by rep-
utable medical research. The construction of the myth of the promotion of homosexuality is effective in part because it is preceded by
the articulation, homosexuality = threat to other elements in the social
. . . AIDS 'hysteria' has generated a great deal of hostility towards les-
bians and gays, from everyday discrimination to 'queer-bashing'. Section 28 gives this expression of hostility an officially sanctioned and
apparently disinterested form . . . The representation of disease as
originating in foreign elements also mobilises the . . . discourse on
immigration . . . [It] is a representation of the threat of subversion in
the figure of the diseased gay male invader, and it offers compensation
for anxieties about subversion by creating a sense of consensus. It is
taken for granted that a space of sexual normalcy exists as the prim-
ordial and natural space, and that, although that space is threatened by
the homosexual invader, it remains for the time being uncontami-
nated. At the same time the supporters [of Section 28] discourse is
contradictory, for it contains a vision of the space of the sexual 'norm'
as already thoroughly contaminated by queer otherness.

(A. M. Smith 1994: 196–200)

Smith (1994) draws upon the analysis of the meanings of disease
developed by Susan Sontag in *AIDS and its Metaphors* (1989).
Sontag considers the connections between fears of 'otherness' (particularly other, non-European cultures) and the fears which are
sometimes associated with disease. This study traces articulation of
the oppositions of same/other, health/disease, heterosexuality/
homosexuality, rationality/irrationality, safety/danger. Smith com-
bines a concern with social antagonisms (in this example in relation
to ethnic and sexual differences) with a recognition of the articulation and disarticulation of meaning in a definite situation. Discourses involve constant struggles for dominance and the
generation of resistance. Identities are therefore accomplished
through struggle but they are never complete for there is no closure
of meaning. The construction of an identity, involves the creation
of a boundary which only makes sense when we consider the relations between the inside and the outside of that identity. Post-
structuralist approaches reconstruct discursive oppositions to make
sense of the way that cultures and identities change. We can understand identities, not by listing their attributes but as defined through
the complex interrelations of discursive oppositions within representations.

What about the body as a contested space? So far we have been
concerned to explore how it is acted upon, and how resistance can

be generated. The relationship between the body and the self is always a tricky one to unravel. Here I focus on one example of how the body can be a contested cultural space, the power relations and representations involved in reproductive technologies. Dion Farquhar (1996) explores the operation of feminist discourses on the practices located around assisted reproductive technologies in relation to 'motherhood' and the female body. Dividing feminist discourses into two types, liberal and fundamentalist, she is able to challenge the assumptions of both. In liberal discourses, the assumption that scientific intervention is emancipatory is criticized for celebrating the capacity of androcentric medicine to repair the natural processes at work in the female body. In fundamentalist discourses, however, technological intervention is vilified and the fertility treatments are portrayed as reducing female bodies to the status of assembly line objects in a baby factory system. According to Farquhar (1996), both discourses assume the connection between naturalness, femininity and motherhood is incontrovertible. In their place, she makes a plea for the recognition of maternity as a set of diverse historically and socially specific practices which do not fit in with the universalizing tendencies of both liberal and fundamentalist discourses. Drawing upon Donna Haraway's (1991) concept of 'the cyborg', as a discursive hybrid of machine and organism, as a more fruitful metaphor for acknowledging the complexity of human experiences and desires, Farquhar (1996) attempts to explore a range of new parental possibilities. The body is exposed as a discursive space for regulating the meaning of the interconnections between the organic and the technological. Moreover it is one which also treats the organic/technological as a leaky distinction which tells us more about the role of such devices in disarticulating/rearticulating elements of ethical, socio-legal and medical discourses than it can tell us about the body itself. The metaphor of the cyborg thus acts as a disrupter to the operation of leaky distinctions.

What lessons can we draw from these post-structuralist approaches? One significant step would be to consider how social researchers can enter into a dialogue with their readers (both within and beyond the academy). This means that they should treat the reader as a discerning and critical respondent rather than as a sponge for absorbing the stories distributed by authoritative experts. We are also led to question the ideas of originality and authorship and to think about the key concepts of science such as

truth, progress and reason as discursive constructs. Post-structuralist discourse analysis undermines the idea that language is a transmission device for carrying the intention of the author, with the
reader trusting an authoritative voice. Instead, if the author is no
longer the authoritative voice of truth and authenticity, these audiences can be seen as participating in the production of meaning, by
constructing their own stories.

The problem with such theories as explanations of cultural
relations and processes is that the focus is so narrowly directed at
broad overarching systems of representation and general conclusions about the regulation of identities that the spontaneous and
innovative features of the production of meaning have been lost.
There is too much of a fixation on control in Foucault's writings and
too great a concern to explore the realms of high culture in much
of post-structuralist theorizing to provide an adequate framework
for understanding developments in popular culture. However,
these concepts offer useful ways of rethinking the production of
meaning, the role of discourses and the construction of identities.
In addition, the treatment of the body as a contested space offers a
way of expanding the boundaries of popular cultural studies to
include the growth in interest in fashion as well as body art and
body modification.

On the importance of things

So far, we have concentrated on cultural texts as illustrations of the
study of culture in order to draw comparisons between the issues
raised in the study of culture and social scientific practice in general.
Here we broaden the ambit by investigating how cultural artefacts
can be understood but largely as a way of posing new questions
about what social inquiry could be like. The study of material
objects has a long history in design and decorative arts. It is only
since the 1970s that the study of 'material cultures' has begun to
take some shape, although this remains one of the most transdisciplinary areas of research arising from departments of sociology,
cultural studies, anthropology, fashion and design studies. The
diversity of things that could qualify as areas of investigation have
made it a difficult field to define. It includes studies of shopping,
furniture, ornaments and jewellery, gardens, building design,
Tupperware, radio soundscapes, electronic goods (such as the Sony
Walkman), fitted kitchens, album covers, gardens, toys and clothes.

Advocates of material culture studies have certainly had a hard time ensuring that such objects of analysis are taken seriously by social researchers in established disciplines, who have ignored or, worse, disparaged such work as trivial and unscientific. Nevertheless, the identification of the cultural significance of many mundane objects and the emphasis on the uses of artefacts in everyday life provide a framework for rethinking the production of meaning in definite conditions. Early attempts to theorize material objects tended to fall into the trap of building an overarching general theory, whereby the distinctions identified in one area of investigation were regarded as homologous with those elsewhere. In this way class location (or perhaps gender) could be identified as being at work in the distinctions of taste made across artefacts as diverse as food and clothes. So, in this approach, the dispositions within the habitus are portrayed as grounded in class or gender relations. Since the habitus acts as a matrix of perceptions, appreciations and actions, qualitative research methods seem more appropriate. Ethnographic studies of material culture have since demonstrated that the motives for acquiring, possessing and valuing artefacts are enormously varied. As Daniel Miller (1998) argues, the question of which things matter was addressed in anthropology as being the prerogative of the researcher not the people being studied. Miller does not want to fall into a neo-positivist dependence on the people being studied to identify what should be taken seriously but argues that the role of social scientists should be to establish connections between the knowledge produced and lived experiences of those being studied. This attempt to find a balance between detachment and involvement ensures that the complexity of everyday life has some chance of finding its way into the published records of cultural studies and social science (Miller 1998).

If we explore an example of material cultures, such as the study of the suburban icon of Tupperware by Alison J. Clarke (1997), we can see how this approach can yield useful knowledge. As a postwar artefact, Tupperware became an emblem of private consumption. The streamlined and rationally designed artefacts were able to tap into established 'rituals of etiquette and socialization associated with food and entertainment within the home' (Clarke 1997: p. 135). Drawing on Miller, Clarke identifies how the relationship of the artefact to cultural relations, as a mechanism for social gatherings combining selling with party games, was crucial in ensuring its presence in many suburban homes. Moreover, Tupperware

could establish a presence without disturbing the acquiescence of
women in occupying the domestic role of so-called 'normal' family
life. According to Clarke:

> Tupperware was constructed not as an occasional household imple-
> ment but as a 'method' of substantiating and expanding the values of
> everyday civility. This synthesis of materiality and spirituality is at the
> crux of what historians have described as 'the Puritan aesthetic'; a
> notion, some have argued, crucial to the formation of American his-
> tory and mass consumption.
>
> (Clarke 1997: 137)

The Tupperware marketing strategy is not explainable in purely
rational economic terms, for it generated a complex network which
mixed caring, nurturing and belonging (securing self-respect and
countering the isolation of suburban women) with sound business
sense. To understand the interconnections between these forms of
production and consumption we need to address the meanings of
such artefacts through their uses in everyday life, not just their aesthetic modernist design. This consideration of the appropriation of
commodities as objects of desire has much in common with the
approach developed by Michel de Certeau. While Bourdieu
analysed the inscription of meaning in texts, for de Certeau meaning is produced through use. De Certeau, who has been described
as both a cultural historian and a cultural geographer, argues that
commercial practices are written into the practices of everyday life
and we should not always look at the most obvious locations (the
advertising and the glossy packaging of a product). Whereas Bourdieu is caught up with the prospect for delineating the popular aesthetic (with its harsh and brash appeals to vulgarity and bodily
appetites) and the pure aesthetic (invoking disinterested detachment as the route to aesthetic appreciation of the beautiful), de
Certeau offers a more flexible framework. If meaning is produced
through use, he argues, then subaltern groups can fashion their own
environment through their appropriation of such objects. The
meaning of Tupperware, initially a dinner service accessory, has
been transformed through its appropriation by the informal economy. He describes the process of active reading whereby the reader
takes away only those things that are pleasurable. Moreover, the
positioning of texts and artefacts in the cultural hierarchy can be
changed as demonstrated by textual poaching.

Dominant cultural forms from opera to fine art are subject to a constant struggle between readers and writers. De Certeau (1984) pinpoints the scriptural economy (sometimes referred to as the economy of writing) whereby interpretative agencies, such as critics, attempt to set limits on the many voices and regulate meanings. This operates effectively due to our socialization, that we are trained to look for the author's voice without leaving footprints on the text. Where the audience have been well trained we can see how this might be the case. In one application of this approach to the fanzines that proliferate around comics, films and television programmes within the science fiction genre, Jenkins (1992) identified how the producers of popular cultural texts attempt to close down appropriations by consumers which could harm the brand image (such as adult rated versions of *Star Wars* which would relegate the product to the lower cultural category of pornography). Certainly this approach draws our attention to the complex ways in which audiences pick up, use and discard texts and artefacts and the equally complex informal economy of collectibles which has grown up around the toys and promotional materials tied to film and TV programmes. The characterization of readers as 'nomads poaching their way across fields, despoiling the wealth of Egypt to enjoy it themselves' (de Certeau 1984: 174) underestimates the creativity of audiences.

Two things are missing from this account of the uses of culture. First, the presence of a cultural hierarchy as a fixed inventory goes unchallenged, for poaching only reshuffles the cards in the pack changing the pecking order of cultural texts. Second, the producers and writers are placed in a privileged position while the audience's many uses of the texts and artefacts are characterized as uncoordinated and in some cases fleeting. The argument that readers are rewriting the text seems to have been lost in de Certeau's account. The study of media fandom provides a more rounded approach to popular cultural consumption.

> Media fandom gives every sign of becoming a permanent culture, one which has survived and evolved for more than twenty-five years and has produced material artefacts of enduring interest to that community. Unlike the readers de Certeau describes, fans get to keep what they produce from the materials they poach from mass culture, and these materials sometimes become a limited source of economic profit as well ... many earn enough to pay for their expenses and finance their fan activities. This materiality makes fan culture a fruitful site for studying the tactics of popular appropriation and textual poaching.

> Yet, it must be acknowledged that the material goods produced by
> fans are not simply the tangible traces of transient meanings produced
> by other reading practices. To read them in such a fashion is to offer
> an impoverished account of fan cultural production. Fan texts, be they
> fan writing, art, song, or video, are shaped through the social norms,
> aesthetic conventions, interpretive protocols, technological resources,
> and technical competence of the larger fan community.
>
> (Jenkins 1992: 49)

The emphasis of de Certeau is plainly on the strategies of powerful
cultural producers in centralized media institutions while consumption involves the ad-hoc transgressive tactics of the weak engaging
in resistance (de Certeau 1984: 36–7; Morley and Silverstone 1990;
Morley 1995). So, even though this approach emphasizes the
importance of the uses of cultural texts and artefacts as the source
of meaning, there is still a tendency to privilege the production of
culture over consumption.

Reinventing the object as a cultural artefact: the new task of social science

The post-structuralist concerns with the production of meaning in
a condition of intertextuality has parallels in Hall's (1973) working
through of the problem of the encoding and the decoding of meanings (although they emerged for quite different reasons and in
quite distinctive theoretical problematics). These kinds of affinities
between neo-Marxism and cultural analysis alongside the common
heritage in structuralism drew them into the same orbit. If one
thing remains from Marxism it is the terminology associated with
the production of meaning as largely in terms of struggle and contestation. The acquisition of the idea of articulation broke with the
logic of mediation, a logic which had assumed that culture is a
manifestation of some underlying economic or class foundation.
The emergent post-Marxists needed a new basis for understanding
the relationship between knowledge construction, power relations
and the construction of subject positions. Foucault's approach provided this and helped to emphasize the role of power relations in
culture. For Hall, this approach holds its own dangers, for it has the
potential for absorbing too much into 'discourse'; if the discursive
field is defined in too idealistic a way it can neglect the materiality
of social relations (Hall 1997). So, much depends on how discourse
is understood. Nevertheless, the way we represent such things has

important consequences on the way we think about them. Analogies and metaphors clearly matter in the operation of power/knowledge as well as in the generation of resistance.

What we need then is a way of thinking about social science as a communicative practice, if you like as having a materiality through the institutional practices of disciplinary projects. I shall leave the question of whether we should be oriented towards disciplines for Chapter 6. Nevertheless, if we are to be reflexive practitioners we have to recognize that the rules of conduct we follow and modify, the languages we use, the textual reference points we cite, the values we hold, the cultural relations we inhabit, the way we exclude and include others, all of these are part of the discursive conditions of social inquiry. Moreover, when it comes to communicating findings and developing arguments for a variety of audiences, we can learn a great deal from the cultural theories identified above. The cultural transmission or scriptural economy approaches are tied to the idea of producing readerly works for passive, well socialized and acquiescent audiences. De Certeau (1984) provides a way of thinking about how the economy of writing can affect the material and intellectual resources in a specific cultural location. If we are to avoid falling into tactical responses to strategic forces then we need to recognize that all attempts to close down alternative readings will only be partially effective. This opens up the possibility of rewriting the literature on knowledge we view as canonical by reading it in new ways (certainly reading it in a less deferential way). It also offers the prospect that we can think of ways of writing which are more inclusive and open to rewriting through the act of reading; moving, as Barthes suggested, towards a writerly approach.

There are two sides to this project. First, rereading the authoritative works of social science in order to identify the five codes at work in the readerly text: the hermeneutic code introduces, defines and resolves the social scientific problem within the narrative; the proairetic code on the development of the narrative; the symbolic code made up of oppositions such as truth/falsehood, objectivity/subjectivity and associated codes from ethics and aesthetics which creep into social science behind the backs of those who study factual evidence; the semic code of meanings attached to words or statements and the moral assumptions at work in particular phraseology; the referential code constructing the specific representations of reality beyond the text. This would enable us to recognize the complexity of the text. Second, we should also acknowledge the complex conditions and varied ways in which people use social scientific knowledge. Like the study of culture, the work on the diverse audiences of social inquiry has barely begun. We can define the conditions of communication in various ways, but we cannot escape the role of discourse in constructing social scientific accounts. The question is how do social scientists acknowledge this as part of their research practice and develop a greater sensitivity to the importance of narrative interpretation and storytelling as well as audience reception. In addition, by viewing social scientific knowledge, metaphorically, as an artefact we are forced to address the way that broader audiences than the academy and policy communities live with the products of social scientific research.

6

Culture and the Prospects for a Postdisciplinary Social Science

Limiting the meaning of culture to the projection of a single view-point or a hierarchical pecking order ignores a great deal of what is of interest to a social scientist. For instance, the role of popular culture in social relations appears sometimes to have been trivialized. In addition, the idea that culture is just transmitted in a linear fashion from sender to receiver (like an arrow hitting a target) ignores the ways in which communication involves dialogue between the participants and neglects the varied uses of cultural products. Yet, the cultural dimension of human societies are the most significant areas of contemporary social research. This final chapter brings together two themes running throughout the text:

- questioning 'canonicity' and its effects in the social sciences
- clarifying how social scientific practice is changing in the light of the acknowledgement of the importance of culture.

Critics and satirists have claimed that cultural analysis is somehow less important than the study of the state, the economy and institutions such as education or the criminal justice system. What this ignores, as demonstrated in the previous chapters, is the important cultural dimension in all of these traditional objects of analysis within social research.

The concern with culture in recent social inquiry is more than a shift of focus to new objects; it also means that social scientists have to reassess their own positions. For instance, understanding the operation of governance and the place of democratic states depends upon acknowledging the part played by 'civic culture' and the complex forms taken by cultural politics. In welfare studies and the sociology of education, we can see a consistent concern with the cultures of poverty and the problem of cultural deprivation. However, what has changed is the way that culture is defined. These approaches tended to treat cultural relations as segmented from and subservient to other spheres. In welfare and educational studies, the problems identified were, it was argued, the product of cultural transmission or its failure. The idea that people could invent their own cultures with their own understanding of the social world has often been treated as a threat. Such cultural resistances were categorized as deviant subcultures. Even social research on the economy is now packed full of references to 'enterprise culture', 'corporate culture' and the 'cultures of production'. As illustrated by Clarke's (1997) study of the Tupperware phenomenon, it is not just about goods being sold through the use of cultural symbols and messages. Social scientists now recognize that the study of the cultural dimension is central to understanding actual economies and states. The study of culture had often been subordinated to economic and political explanations even within cultural studies, as the dominance of the frame of reference by political economy has demonstrated. However, we have to acknowledge the double take and recognize that social scientists have often been studying the cultural when they claim to be studying the state, the mind or the economy. In many cases, it was the study of culture by another name. Social scientists draw upon the existing 'repertoires of representation' (within the academic communities and the wider culture they inhabit) when making sense of their chosen area of study, defining concepts, developing arguments and so on. The same is true when engaging in the practice of conducting research and in the presentation of findings for their respective audiences. In short, the social scientist is and always has been a cultural agent. Social scientists use the skills provided by the cultures they inhabit and their chosen objects of analysis are understood through cultural interpretations.

We have experienced two centuries of disciplinarity where the study of the social has presumed that 'objects of analysis' are concrete things with a definite structure or alternatively that they are constituted by a set of components accessible to some procedure of knowing. The plausibility of disciplinary narratives was achieved through the operationalization of the distinction between the normal and the pathological. As a result, social scientific practices have been tied to power relations by translating cultural values into authoritative knowledge. Despite the arguments about the character of social inquiry, the continuities in academic practices over time and across fields of knowledge are constantly emphasized. Yet this continuity has been destabilized during the 1980s and 1990s. In contemporary social science, objects of analysis are increasingly seen as complex, uncertain and contested spaces. Debates on difference and otherness have played a significant role in this. To understand this process, this chapter explores the changes in classificatory practices and judgements involved in contemporary social scientific practices.

Disciplinarity and complexity

Objects of analysis are not what they used to be. Once, so the history of social science tells us, they were secure, fixed, a matter of definition and not in question. Now they are in doubt, problematic, under erasure and without foundation. This does not signify a fundamental change in the social structure. Both the natural and social worlds have always been complex and discursively constituted. We have just been very effective at convincing ourselves that the world is simple, atomistic, a collection of empirical regularities and subject to the whims of phenomenalists and nominalists (who have argued that what we see is what we get and that the names we devise for things are accurate reflections of what they are). As I argue later, it is the adoption of a closed system analysis of the social (see Table 2) which has served to shore up the social science disciplines.

By examining the implication of closed system analysis in the study of people within social relationships and institutions it is possible to establish how the disciplines of sociology, psychology and economics were able to consolidate their professional academic status. Emulating the successful natural sciences through a series of analogies and metaphors offered a fast track to building up trust in the knowledge produced. Science is a very powerful and evocative word or idea in western culture. It conveys legitimacy and authenticity upon the people, ideas and institutions with which it is associated. A claim to authenticity means that a statement is 'true to life',

Table 2 Closed and open systems in the social sciences

	Closed systems	*Open systems*
1 **Simplicity and complexity**	A limited number of measurable variables to increase the possibility of identifying and predicting clear relationships	A state of complexity is acknowledged as the condition of one's objects of analysis and the relations between them
2 **External boundary**	Exclusion clauses ensure that the confusing mass of possible influences are screened out (such as the *ceteris paribus* clause, that holding all other things constant *x* will lead to *y*)	No external boundary is assumed to exist so that each object can be part of multiple causal relations and that one cannot predict an outcome with any degree of certainty
3 **Intrinsic properties**	All objects of analysis are taken at face value so that the intrinsic properties of an object are not considered	Recognition that all objects have intrinsic properties and structures which affect their performance in different conditions

Source: Smith 2000: 45

the real thing rather than an imitation. To be effective, disciplinary projects had to (or have to) engage with a variety of audiences (within the academy, within policy communities and in the public sphere). Disciplinary projects have to establish some degree of plausibility with these audiences so that they come to be seen as authentic accounts of the social world or, at least, a discrete portion of it. In Durkheimian fashion, each discipline sought to construct its own distinctive object of analysis and establish its respective claim to be able to speak authoritatively upon it.

Closure has been an important part of all disciplines which have sought to establish objective knowledge. The assumption that closure can be achieved, whereby extraneous variables can be excluded in order to achieve a 'interference-free' zone for identifying clear-cut relations (conjunctions between empirical variables) remains extremely popular as a technique. How it is applied in different social scientific disciplines depends on how the object of analysis is constructed in each case. If we take the example of political science, the specification of 'the state' and political institutions was also tied to the adoption of behaviourist assumptions about observable concrete decisions and the operation of power. Dahl defined this method as the 'examination of the political relationships of men [*sic*] ... with the object of formulating and testing hypotheses concerning uniformities of behaviour' (Dahl 1961: 764). The treatment of the concept of power as an empirical regularity is observable, measurable and explainable in terms of how the behaviour of one agent causes the behaviour of another, so that the latter does things that they would not otherwise do (Dahl 1957). This approach is limited to researching actual decision-making behaviour by groups of individuals within situations where observable conflict of interests exist. These interests are defined as expressed policy preferences revealed directly through political participation. This means that we should take what political actors say and what they do to be a direct expression of their interests. By focusing upon the specific outcomes of observable behaviour, the pluralist approach is able to gather 'reliable evidence' (which has been subject to further tests and which produces the same or similar results). This usually takes the form of quantitative data in order to facilitate correlations between variables (statistical comparisons). Pluralists used statistical controls to simulate a closed system involving a limited number of simple variables (see Blalock 1964). In effect, in order to establish a plausible scientific approach, the disciplinary project had to construct a 'political subject' which fitted the bill neglecting the actual complexities of political decision making and, as Dahl (1961) came to accept in his later work, regardless of the need to understand the wider cultural conditions of political relations and processes (Smith 2000: ch. 3).

This example draws our attention to the relationship between *what* is known and *how* we know; between our various ontological assumptions and presuppositions about the social world and the epistemological procedures for knowing the social. In the search for plausibility, social scientists have assumed that their simplifications of social processes are a mimetic (reflectionist) account of the way the world operates. It is important to establish what complexity means. In research work on social scientific practice (Smith 1998b: 321), a number of kinds of complexity have been identified.

- *Practical complexity.* This involves recognizing that simple relations are artificial human inventions, for other factors always have a part to play when we are reconstructing social existence (that the empirical world is always much more complex than we expect).

- *Imaginative complexity*. Rather than seeing thoughts as a reflection of the things we study, it is important to recognize the way that imaginative thinking organizes our perceptions, sensations and impressions (that we simplify empirical complexity through imaginative thought).
- *Situated complexity*. All forms of knowledge, including scientific knowledge, are the complex product of the practices established in historical and social locations where they were produced. As such, they carry the cultural values upon which they were grounded although they may be received in other locations in quite different ways.
- *Representational complexity*. That the production of meaning is itself a complex process, composed of linguistic, symbolic and cultural elements, all of which can have dramatic affects on how social scientists construct evidence and communicate arguments to others.
- *Structural or deep complexity*. That in order to see science as an intelligible activity, the things we study must have real internal properties (real powers and liabilities) but that our only way of expressing these things is through representation.

Each kind of complexification involves a further step away from the conventional view of what it means to be scientific. If we accept that studying people involves acknowledging these aspects of social complexity then we must also acknowledge that the adoption of a closed system approach is inappropriate. Disciplinarity and the preference for closure are closely related to the desire for authoritative knowledge. To go further, we have to have a clear idea of what disciplinarity means as a conceptual tool. Two closely connected dimensions stand out, drawing together the points made in earlier chapters.

The *discursive dimension* highlights the unifying characteristic of a discipline – its capacity for self-reference and self-regulation (autopoiesis). Disciplinary discourses are effective to the extent that they provide a framework within which meanings can be regulated. They attempt to shut down the possibility of alternative interpretations by drawing upon the stock of common-sense knowledge which has come to be accepted. Discourses regulate the production of meaning with reference to an established set of textual sources (often canonized) and within the institutional practices through which we classify people. One way in which this is achieved is by directly tapping into tacit prejudices, values and taken-for-granted assumptions about cultural differences. For a disciplinary discourse to work, the use of language also has to be organized through good storytelling (McCloskey 1983) enabling its deployment within the inclusionary and exclusionary relations of everyday life. This is achieved through the construction of subject positions. However, this kind of strategy to fix meaning is never completely successful for audiences can produce meanings in unanticipated ways and people can even resist the systems of classification involved as well as the ways in which they are classified.

The *knowledge dimension* indicates the important role played by social scientists as cultural agents. Since we can never be separate from the things we study (the language systems and specific cultural values, the rules of conduct informing social practices and the institutional and textual conditions of knowledge production), then the best position we can maintain is to acknowledge this condition and try to be aware of the way we draw upon and articulate classificatory systems in order to engage in classificatory practices (the location of things in categories). Earlier I argued, by drawing upon Bourdieu's (1984) analysis of the way 'taste classifies the classifier', that in social science, the attachment to markers of authenticity like validity, reliability, rationality, truth and progress are just as important. Social science also has its carefully maintained stable reference points through which we can recognize an 'authoritative' intervention, using the accepted rhetorical formula. The distinctions that operate within knowledge construction serve as a measure of value. As a result, social scientific texts and practices often attempt to mimic the 'authoritative voice', embodying the cultural heritage of a specific time and place for a specific audience.

Power relations are an inherent part of the way social scientific practice is conducted. The kinds of knowledge produced through social science operate through the normalizing and pathologizing of different kinds of behaviour and identities. The plausibility of disciplinary narratives has been achieved through the operationalization of the distinction between the normality and pathology, articulating, mobilizing and reinventing prejudices. As a result, social scientific practices have been tied to power relations by translating cultural values into authoritative knowledge. While the normalizing and pathologizing tendencies of social scientific practices are now open to question the experience across the social sciences has varied. To explore this further, we shall briefly consider three areas of social research – cultural geography, social psychology and the study of crime and deviance.

Disciplinarity under erasure: identity, space and place

In the area of social research now defined as cultural geography, we can find a useful demonstration of the impact of cultural theory on social scientific practice. Cultural geography considers the formation of identities in relation to space and place. The way we see ourselves in relation to the places where we live, work and play is itself a complex product of the boundaries we construct between ourselves and others. The kinds of boundaries we draw have had an impact through the inclusion and exclusion of others. Think of the territorial boundaries in Northern Ireland between Catholic and Protestant peoples, boundaries which have been marked with symbolic representations and artefacts such as murals or the 'peace wall'. In the northern towns of England, social classes were distributed in distinctive housing estates signifying relative status and levels of affluence. At a more familiar level, we can see this in the uses of walls and fences (or even the strategically placed potted plant) as garden artefacts for maintaining boundaries between notional private spaces. These boundaries and the precise characteristics of the artefacts are articulated with differing concepts of neighbourliness. To give a 'place' meaning, we also draw upon the kinds of oppositions discussed earlier, such as same/other, friend/stranger, security/danger, masculinity/femininity, and so on. In this way, we produce the meaning of places and the boundaries between them in our everyday lives. Cultural geography also assumes that 'culture' involves constant struggles for dominance and the generation of resistance through which identities are accomplished.

The post-structuralist approach to discourse and identity has generated new insights into the idea of 'place' in the disciplinary field of human geography (see Massey 1994, 1995). More recently, the application of such approaches to the environment has begun to transform social research on physical geography. This concern with culture is not new as is often thought but draws upon the writings of Yi-Fu Tuan (1974, 1978, 1984), who has been exploring the meaning of the landscape and the relationship between the 'social' and 'natural' in phenomenological terms since the 1960s. With the waning of the dominance of quantitative geography in the 1970s and the subsequent failure of the political economy approach to fill the gap in the 1980s, the concern with cultural interpretation has had the space to flourish. Initially this approach has focused on the foundational myths associated with mapping and demonstrated the ethnocentricity of the ways in which we image space and place. While Tuan adopted a more empirical approach, his account also considers the role of oppositional relations. These included life/death, male/female, we/they and how they related to land/water, centre/periphery, north/south, high/low, heaven/earth and so on. It went on to explore the complex cultural representations of landscapes and human relationships within them (Tuan 1974).

Recent research has focused on and criticized the foundational stories that provide the 'origin myths' of urban landscapes. That cities had some underlying plan and purpose when they are more adequately understood as spatial phenomena within which a variety of stories, rhythms, movements and networks coexist and which have varying levels of interaction and quite distinct space-times. This shift in geographical analysis is expressed in the writings of Doreen Massey.

> Cities, both individually and in the relations between them, are spatial phenomenon. On immediate reading, this might seem to be blindingly obvious. Of course cities *are* spatial: they are spaces, they exist *in* space. These things are true but we mean something more than this. For one thing there has been a sea-change within the social sciences in how space itself is conceptualized. Increasingly, the spaces through which we live our lives and through which the world – the cities – come to be organized are understood as social products, and social products formed out of the relations which exist between people, agencies, institutions and so forth.
>
> (Massey 1999: 159)

Cities are heterogeneous terrains containing varying levels of intensity of interaction and varying patterns of mobility, sociability/anonymity, community/difference, order/disorder. Despite a long history of formulating urban planning the result is always much more complex and heterogeneous than expected and cities are likely to become more so. By tracing the role of oppositions within representations of place we can see how same/other and masculine/feminine work together to construct complex ways of defining

identities in places. We can only make sense of identities, not by listing their attributes, but when we see them as defined through the
relations between insiders and outsiders. In this way, places and
boundaries, as well as identities, can also be seen as contested
through the complex interrelations of discursive oppositions. By
recognizing discursive oppositions and by being aware about how
they operated through power relations we are able to make sense
of the way that cultures and identities change.

Cultures, identities and the boundaries used to mark the differences between them constantly shift through the dynamic practices
of human beings which organize and reorganize the built environment and their relationship to it. Using the arguments developed
by de Certeau (1984), Pile and Thrift (1995) suggest that all stories
are, in effect, travel stories whereby the physical mobility of the
body and the use of speech have produced variety of spatial-
symbolic metaphors (such as walking and travelling, even being
nomadic or a tourist). The uses of spatial and body metaphors
abound in cities. Phrases like 'across the tracks' operate as lived
boundaries between safe and dangerous places. Unruly cities are
also described as sick, subject to contagion, disordered and pathological. The articulation of city stories through the identification of
specific problem groups is commonplace – 'blame it on the ghetto'.
Take Johannesburg in South Africa as an example: here the changing urban environment is described as dishevelled and in decay; city
life is frequently represented as 'stressed out'. The flight of economic capital from the city in the 1990s is usually attributed to the
impact of post-Apartheid migrants from other African countries.
The problems of Johannesburg have become a site for the reconstruction of South African national identity. In an effort to unify
many peoples and languages, every television programme link
carries representatives of at least two South African peoples. Every
advertising hoarding carries the new nation message (even station-
ery suppliers are 'addressing the nation'). The fabrication of a non-
racist South Africa with relations of equivalence and sameness has
been achieved at the cost of stigmatizing other black Africans as
the cause of the nation's ills; racism has been replaced by xeno-
phobia. Johannesburg has been articulated as the epitome of the
problem.

The foundational stories of cities also simplify the relationship
between the social and the natural, that cities are represented as
displacements of nature with clear lines of demarcation between

them. Steve Hinchcliffe (1999) argues that a more adequate approach should accommodate the presence of complex relations between urban wildlife and the green spaces which can flourish in urban spaces. Instead we should focus on city-nature formations grounded in distinctive sets of ethical practices regulating the use of land or as to the appropriate relationship between human and non-human animals. In order to accommodate the range of cultural practices involved in the shifting patterns of agricultural use and market gardening within urban centres, the preservation of urban wildlife sites, the conversion of derelict landscapes and so on, we need a more flexible conceptual framework than that provided by the resort to the urban/rural divide (with its connotations of the distinction between association and community, respectively).

We also need to avoid falling into the subdisciplinary trap of focusing on one or the other for so-called rural experiences are just as complex and shot through as urban ones. Massey argues that 'places' only make sense within boundaries and these boundaries only make sense when we recognize the complex, changing and uncertain patterns of social existence on both sides of the boundary. The recognition of culture in human geography also has implications for the discipline. In the 1940s, Alfred Schütz was introduced as a sociologist at an academic meeting to which one person responded: 'What kind of sociologist are you, urban or rural?' Such distinctions can be catching. We should be sensitive to how social scientists draw upon the existing repertoires of representation (within the academic communities and the wider culture they inhabit) in their chosen area of study. Social scientists study things using the skills provided by the cultures they inhabit. Their chosen objects of analysis are also defined and understood through embedded cultural assumptions.

Disciplinarity in doubt: the mind as a contested space

Recent research in social psychology has attempted to build bridges with sociological cultural approaches. Discursive psychology offers a research programme which provides significant opportunities for interactionist, phenomenological and ethnomethodological branches of sociology to assimilate in a reasonably unproblematic way. This approach to discourse is more empirical than the post-structuralist one discussed earlier for it offers ways of understanding everyday social interaction in the construction of meanings. But it is also sensitive to the use of representations, analogy and metaphor in the study of communication as an ongoing dynamic process. In particular, the use of Rom Harré's account of the body as a site for 'grounding our personal identities . . . as points of reference in relating to material things . . . for the assignment of all sorts of roles, tasks, duties and strategies' (Harré 1991: 257) provides a useful benchmark in highlighting the dialogue between disciplinary fields. Discursive psychology is concerned to establish how meanings are produced through practically oriented interactions. The sense of 'practical' used here appears to draw loosely from Giddens' (1982a, 1982b) description of practical knowledge as containing capability (that the actors involved have the motive and resources to engage and sustain interaction) and knowledgeability (that they can monitor their own activities within the knowledge system they inhabit).

In terms of active research practice, discursive psychology has been concerned to explore the meanings generated through conversations and documents from everyday life. This way of defining discourse is similar to the ways in which conventionalist approaches to scientific knowledge consider the role of scientific language within organized academic communities (Keat and Urry 1978; Smith 1998b: ch. 5). However, discursive psychologists have placed a strong emphasis upon the role of active communication in the production of meanings. Conversational analysis explores the relations between speakers, their surroundings, their shared experiences and intentions, the event of which conversation is a part, even the pauses, silences and the 'umms' and 'errs' which are often overlooked but which are just as much a part of the experience of communication. Rather than viewing attitudes as the product of cognitive structures, they have been reinterpreted as evaluative assessments which contain a whole series of implicit clues and hints. As a consequence, this approach has developed into an extensive qualitative research programme in the field of knowledge often defined as Critical Psychology (Potter and Wetherell 1987; Edwards and Potter 1993). Like the approaches discussed earlier, 'discourse' is a product of the ways in which people produce meaning by drawing upon the rules of language and its conduct. Within the broader field of psychology, the things which have been taken as given in the past – such as causes and facts – have been subject to intense scrutiny. These things have been transformed from a resource into a topic for research. Discursive psychology is therefore not posing a different set of objects of analysis for the discipline to take seriously, it is suggesting that the existing objects of analysis can be understood in a very different way (Harré and Gillett 1994).

Within the field one text seems to serve as a common point of reference for the various approaches. Jonathan Potter and Margaret Wetherell's (1987) analysis of discourse as the activity of talking and writing draws upon a variety of sources in a transdisciplinary way in much the same way as many approaches considered earlier. They select approaches and good ideas to work through the problems of analysis they have encountered in active research. As a result, they have drawn from the semiology of Barthes and the qualitative methodology (as well as the focus on taken-for-granted common-sense assumptions which serve as the conditions of communication) from ethnomethodology. In addition, they draw upon John Austin's (1962) 'speech act' theory on the use of words as deeds. Potter and Wetherall (1987) argue that one of the key characteristics of the uses of language is how it involves doing things, that it has purposes and intentions. As a consequence of their research activities they came to realize that certain types of speech acts can follow in sequence so as to create loose rule-governed situations (such as conversations). The sense of 'rule-governed' here refers to those flexible rules operating largely tacitly and which have to be constantly renegotiated to respond to the uncertainties involved in human activities. In order to explain how the general structural level relates to everyday speech they drew upon the ethogenic approach of Rom Harré which distinguished between competence and performance. Competence involves having a command of a particular language system, knowing its rules of conduct and working within them in order to communicate with others. Therefore, it involves the possession of a set of skills, understandings and values which can be drawn upon in the activity of speaking or writing in definite situations. Performance activates communication skills in order to engage in social inter-action (Harré and Secord 1973; Harré 1979; Harré and Gillett 1994). We should remember that this approach was not developed with the responses of sociologists in mind but the audiences well versed in the assumptions of the behaviourist and cognitive psychologies. To be persuasive with this audience, they had to touch base with widely recognized psychological explanations, reinterpreting them in the process.

This approach sees the role of representations as playing an active constructive role in the formation of the world. However, this approach does not fix representations to predefined communities. This would mean that groups could be used to define the scope of the conventions and representations with which we are concerned but they do not match in such a neat way (Potter and Wetherell 1987: ch. 7). In order to provide a more open-ended and flexible approach to discourse and representation, they develop the idea of an 'interpretive repertoire' (drawing from Mulkay 1991). This refers to collections of ideas, concepts and terms which are used to define and evaluate experiences and events. Discursive psychology also tries to bridge the gap between theoretical and empirical accounts of communication as well as exploring the lived experience of communication between people with intentions and purposes, a feature which is absent from many examples of poststructuralist analysis for this presumes a knowing subject (a category that post-structuralism would place in question).

This is not the only kind of discursive psychology to emerge. The Bolton Discourse Network (BDN) have identified how this approach can be applied in more varied ways, akin to the emergence of the material cultures stream in cultural studies. The BDN have tried to widen the preoccupations of discourse analysis beyond textual and conversational analysis establishing a stronger connection with those areas of cultural studies which explore visual representations such as advertising and comics as well as the body, organizations, cities and gardens (defined as physical texts). Earlier, one of the founder members of the BDN, Ian Parker (1992), attempted to develop a critical response to discursive psychology drawing upon the misleading conceptual game of 'rationality vs. relativism'. This is misleading, because it sets up an unsustainable contrast; even relativists make universal claims (Harré and Krausz 1996). Perhaps the most effective challenge is the methodological critique of discursive psychology for focusing too narrowly on conversational and textual evidence in the empirical sense; neglecting the assumptions and values which underpin communication and representation, the shared tacit knowledge which acts as the conditions of possibility so that communication can do its work. More recently, Parker (1999) appears to have adopted a more conciliatory approach to discursive psychology.

The gradual merging of critical realist with discursive concerns in this area offers one model for moving away from disciplinarity. Parker *et al.* (1995) focused attention on the need to deconstruct psychopathology as a situated practice, directly challenging the role of experts in mental health practice, whether they are therapists, psychiatrists or psychologists. This is achieved through careful consideration of oppositional distinctions at work in the diagnosis of specific conditions (reason/unreason, lay/professional, individual/social, form/content, categories/messy real life and last but not least, normality/pathology). Along similar lines, Erica Burman *et al.* (1996) have offered a detailed exploration of the role of therapeutic practices in the construction of subject positions. However, as critical psychologists they want to make a difference. Thus they also point to the ways in which therapeutic practices (from educational psychology to gender identity therapists) open up opportunities for resistance by patients to the pathologizing tendencies of professional experts. The discourses of psychiatry and psychology attempt to regulate the production of meaning yet they are always open to destabilization, subversion and can even facilitate empowerment.

One of the most important areas of concern in psychological research on culture has been explaining the uses of racist stereotypes. The categorizations of groups according to 'race' are manufactured through the constant repetition and reformulation of narratives and stories constructed in everyday life. The close relationship between ethnocentric bias in psychopathological and psychiatric research and their role in defining culturally specific behaviour as abnormal and hence in need of treatment and/or detainment has been identified in a number of studies (for examples see Fernando *et al.* 1997; Littlewood and Lipsedge 1997). Discursive psychology has attempt to understand the unacknowledged conditions of racist values within situated conversations and texts (as well as in psychological knowledges).

Judgements about cultural differences and the associated values involve the operationalization of complex classification procedures which are to some extent shared and serve as the tacit basis for producing meanings. These approaches are, in their different ways, very effective in exploring the rules of conduct which permit particular kinds of offensive talk and indiscretions. What discursive psychology appears to lack is an adequate basis for theorizing its account of the modes of classification which organize and regulate what meanings can or cannot be produced. The difficulty here is that discursive psychology contends with the strong disciplinary identity of mainstream psychology, which is heavily committed to the adoption of 'scientific techniques' and closed system analysis; the disciplinary project assumes that entry into the profession involves careful socialization in these preferred methods. In the next case study, we will look at the disciplinary field in which psychopathology and psychiatry play a performing role, the discipline of criminology. In this example, I want to stress the resilience of disciplinarity in social inquiry.

Disciplinarity largely intact: the (re-)construction of criminal subjects

The discursive regulation mechanisms which have been problematized and challenged in sociology, cultural studies, geography and, to a lesser extent, in psychology retain their efficacy in the study of crime. Throughout this text, I have argued that the effectivity of a disciplinary project rests as much with being plausible to its audiences as with the capacity of criminology to ensure that researchers pursue the party line on the purpose of their field of knowledge. Indeed, criminology has managed not only to produce a huge variety of causal explanations of criminal behaviour and its origin but also to withstand a variety of concerted critical barrages by sociologists and social psychologists since the 1960s for doing exactly this. The continual process of turning over one causal explanation after another does not seem to have caused doubt and critical reflection on the operation of the discipline. The distinguishing feature of this area of social research is the capacity to translate complex personal histories and associated social experiences into psychological conditions, syndromes, disorders and malfunctions. Once I have outlined some examples of the succession of criminal subjects, I shall suggest two possible reasons for this state of affairs based on the previous arguments.

The study of crime provides us with a useful terrain to consider the role of disciplinary discourses when they have been especially successful at regulating the production of meaning. First, unlike some areas of inquiry, it provides a terrain where all the social sciences have contributed. Indeed, some of the most important contributions to the study of crime have been one-off interventions by social theorists and researchers from other areas of work. Second, there is a central core of social research, the discipline of criminology, which attempts to generate a disciplinary project around the task of identifying the causes of criminality. The hard core of the disciplinary project draws heavily from psychology but has come into contact with writers from sociology, politics and economics, each leaving its own legacy. This disciplinary project has attempted to establish firm foundations for a particular subject position, the 'criminal subject'. However, as soon as we explore specific discourses on criminality, we can see how the cultural norms specific to a time and place are articulated with distinctive ethical rules. It is in the ethico-cultural mix that we can make sense of the shifting expectations on what constitutes transgressive or appropriate behaviour in a specific location.

In the development of the various approaches within the history of criminology we can see a sequence of criminal subjects articulated within the criminological discourses. It is through such subjects that knowledge of the violation of social norms can be understood both within the criminal justice system and beyond. In each case, the 'criminal subject' is constructed in a way which matches the system of representation at work in the criminological discourses concerned. Hence, the people convicted of illegal actions are punished within the rules of conduct, established texts and institutions which make sense of the world through these discourses. For example, in utilitarian accounts of crime the 'criminal subject' is a rational decision maker who responds to an appropriate punishment prescribed for each criminal action in law. However, the positivist 'criminal subject' is imagined to have a disposition towards committing crime as well as definite propensities for reform. In this positivist criminological discourse, where criminals have different ways of responding to different punishments, the punishment should fit the criminal rather than the crime. In each social scientific discipline, we can find a range of 'subjects' constructed by the competing perspectives within each field of knowledge. These subjects, these imaginary figures of disorder and violation through which discourses are given coherence and relevance for those who invest in them, are constructed as much within the sociology of deviance (or sociology in general) as within the criminal justice system.

A short and truncated overview of the succession of criminal subjects is useful for our purposes here. The so-called Classical School of criminology came into existence through the work of Cesare de Beccaria (1764/1963), who drew upon Enlightenment liberal social contract theory. Beccaria argued for the severity of punishment to match the crime rather than the personage and standing of the offender. This was stimulated by the excesses that resulted from the emergence of police forces and the growth of penal regimes throughout Europe in the eighteenth century. In particular, Beccaria was scathing of the police in Paris for their intervention in response to moral and political opinion as well as in crime. His publications (at first anonymously) challenged the use of arbitrary power and urged consistency in the application of legal codes. Nevertheless, in the standard histories of penology, the humanitarian aspect of his work is overstated for he accepted the need for corporal punishment and judicial torture (Newman and Marongui 1990). In Britain, Jeremy Bentham also outlined how the felicific calculus could be used to deter the hedonistic tendencies of individuals. Both approaches were concerned to deter yet the characterization of the criminal subject by Beccaria is one where the motives are automatic and completely bound by a web of determination: 'recalcitrant objects who must be angled, steered and forced into law abiding behaviour' (Beirne 1991: 812). This approach secured legitimacy for the criminalization of the emerging urban populations throughout western Europe.

The development of positivist criminology in the 1870s led to a shift in the characterization of the criminal subject . It also led to the attribution of the label of the Classical School to the aforementioned criminologies. For Cesare Lombroso (1876/1911), the causal basis for establishing criminality could be established through the physiological characteristics of the prison population. This account combined phrenology (the study of skull shapes) with other anatomical stigmata (physiological features which supposedly differed from the norm) such as webbed feet, large jaws, large ears, skin colour, thick hair, the inability to blush, the possession of an extra nipple and diminished sensitivity to pain. The attribution of criminality and moral degeneracy to epilepsy ensured that this particular disability became the object of intense interventions by eugenicists. Lombroso used evidence from the crania of 383 dead and 3,839 living criminals to construct a model for predicting the criminal tendencies of the population as a whole (Lombroso 1876/1911). Underlying the construction of the criminal subject was the assumption that criminals were throwbacks to an earlier stage of evolution – dehumanizing as well as pathologizing those concerned. Similarly, he attributed female prostitution to the possession of a big toe somewhat separated from the other toes (Lombroso and Ferrero 1895/1915). The focus on exterior 'signs' of an underlying constitutional disorder would, he argued, deliver a capacity for distinguishing the chronic recidivists from those amenable to reform. Gradually, by the start of the twentieth century, the moralizing elements of criminological discourses came to be subsumed within 'scientific' explanations of pathologies.

As the search for biological determinants came under question in the early twentieth century, criminological theories were supplemented by social determinations. Cyril Burt, later well known for his influence on educational policy and claims about his fraudulent research on intelligence, made his name in British criminology, specifically on juvenile delinquency. Indeed, in discussing crime he was probably the first to attribute a causal basis for media effects in this area. His affable descriptions and storytelling mode yielded a large audience among those working in the British penal system. The publication of *The Young Delinquent* (Burt 1925/1961) had an enormous impact on the treatment of young offenders throughout much of the twentieth century in Britain. Burt's account of criminal inheritance is worth a little further scrutiny. Using genotype analysis, he pinpointed the patterns of pathologies which existed in the families of his case studies and argued that inherent propensities to criminality were potentially controllable if spotted in the very young. In the systematic research work of the team led by W. H. Sheldon (1949), this explanation achieved a new level of sophistication. Using evidence on the social and physical characteristics of young men who had opted for military service rather than prison, Sheldon (1949) explored the relationship between physique and propensity for crime. In this case, he used the photographs taken as part of the military identification procedures in order to classify the bodies as physical types and matched this with social service, medical, psychiatric documents in order to identify patterns of behaviour. He discovered that a series of agencies had conducted investigations to monitor the social background of those examined in the study. Look more closely and you find a wealth of subjective judgements masquerading as factual indicators of pathology. The case studies are numbered, further objectifying the individuals concerned as representative of a type. For example, 'Number 29' has a 'highly energised, extroverted, dramatic sociability', a 'shrewd successful thief' probably destined for 'big time crime' who 'picks up Freudian and Christian profanity like a sponge'. 'Number 34' is remarkable for his gnarled physique, loudness, hair trigger temper and his love of nudity. In each case family background is considered for its difference from the norm. The young men are classified through a complex set of factors organized within the terms of reference of the opposition of the normal and the pathological. Whether the causes of criminality are seen as biogenic, the product of anomie, the consequence of status deprivation or subcultural norms or one's ecological location, each 'criminal subject' has been pathologized. All of these explanations have figured in the late twentieth century at one point or another, although recently the descriptive language has focused upon glandular problems, attention deficit disorders, genetic predispositions and inconsistent parenting.

In each of the previous cases, the 'criminal subject' is constructed in a manner which matches the system of representation at work in the criminological discourses concerned and the wider cultural context. People convicted of illegal actions are punished within the context of rules of conduct, established texts and institutions which make sense of the world through these discourses. Recent criminology appears to be broadly consistent with these attempts to establish patterns of pathological behaviour but differs in one important way. In contemporary accounts of pathologies, however, the focus on clinical assessment of the individual has given way to the 'language of probabilistic calculations' and investigation into the statistical propensity of population groups towards criminality. These new criminologies are concerned more with managing subpopulations and maintaining public safety. The language of these new discourses draws from systems analysis and social utility. In the UK, proposals to detain 'seriously disturbed individuals' (without an offence actually being committed) have been justified by the Blair administration in terms of the balance of probabilities, risk and public safety. This actually reinforces the function of clinical judgement in identifying potentially dangerous forms of behaviour and personality traits. In relation to penal policy, one figure which has featured in the construction of criminal subjects to date – the individualized 'chronic recidivist' – has begun to disappear from penal discourses. According to Malcolm Feeley and Jonathan Simon:

> Instead of social norms like the elimination of crime, reintegration into the community, or public safety, institutions begin to measure their own outputs as indicators of performance. Thus courts may look at docket flow. Similarly, parole agencies may shift evaluations to, say, the time elapsed between arrests and due process hearings.
>
> (Feeley and Simon 1992: 456)

So the processing of people in an efficient manner (something that can be controlled) becomes the measure of performance, just as educational performance is increasingly measured by conducting standardized tests rather than the outputs of certain levels of literacy and numeracy. If reoffending became a measure of performance then they would be unlikely to achieve any targets. Feeley and Simon suggest that this has led to the introduction of new forms of custodial control (such as electronic tagging and curfews for persistent offenders) instead of rehabilitation strategies (Feeley and Simon 1992: 457). As a consequence, the discourses on criminality and penology are now in transformation. Whether they will be consolidated into a new unified disciplinary project or become part of a wider managerialist discourse concerned with public policy is uncertain.

What we can conclude is that we should not ignore the complex relationship between discourses and institutional practices. Earlier, in Chapter 5, we saw Foucault (1980) demonstrate how the links between power/knowledge are very effective. If active and generalized (perhaps largely tacit) consent exists, discourses can work smoothly as systems of domination as well as representation through the rules of conduct, texts and institutional practices where meaning is produced. We should bear in mind that power always generates its own forms of resistance and if meanings are produced in this way, they can also be subverted and changed. Any attempt to destabilize the emergent discourses of crime also has to address the way they organize knowledge and how they are connected to more general discourses constructing social problems.

Now, to return to the objectives raised earlier in this section. Disciplinarity can survive considerable criticism and extended attempts at subversion when the discipline places excessive emphasis on trusting one's own cultural values as foundation for building authoritative knowledge. While criminological discourses have paid lip-service to the belief that scientific evidence separated questions of fact from normative issues, the evidence of value-laden research in this area points to an incredible list of truths falling away in quick succession. The few studies identified here have been selected to highlight the range of approaches in criminology. Faith in the scientific project and/or the moralizing mission of criminological discourses can make for short memories. Moreover, each approach demonstrates gendered and ethnocentric values at work, accepted as tacit knowledge in the research community but rearticulated in each transition.

Criminology also has an institutional presence in the criminal justice system which may mean that it is shielded from wider shifts in academic debate. The established texts of this discipline have served as the reference points for institutional diagnosis, treatment and management throughout the nineteenth and twentieth centuries. It has been consistently and heavily funded by research councils despite periods of funding restraint in other areas. Even during the 1980s, criminological research on the causes and prevention of crime did not experience the same cuts experienced in other areas of the social sciences. In addition, direct funding through the Home Office (in the UK) and the agencies under its supervision have also sustained the disciplinary project. Even governments committed to redefining social problems as personal difficulties (as demonstrated by neo-liberal and some Christian democrat administrations throughout the western world) saw value in maintaining the funding of criminological research. In addition, criminological knowledge not only generates 'good newsworthy copy in the press', but also has been represented in the public sphere in a manner which emphasizes its role as the source of readerly texts. This discipline has been privileged in a variety of ways and it has retained its confidence in the search for certainty despite the self-doubt expressed throughout social and even the natural sciences.

Disciplinarity, interdisciplinarity and postdisciplinarity: cultural analysis as a catalyst

The strong continuities in academic practices acquired through the adoption of closed system analysis to study the social world (although this was achieved in slightly different ways; see Smith 1998b: chs 1–3) carry a price tag. This includes the loss of an awareness of complexity and diversity in objects of analysis. Disciplinary fields of knowledge are tied to the emergence of particular forms of governance in the institutions of the academy. It is useful to explore the distinction between disciplinarity and its alternatives in bold terms

- The institutionalization of *disciplinary knowledge* is the key problem in social science for it generates a narrow focus on one ring-fenced area of concern often producing one-sided accounts of the social. In particular, it ignores important lessons which have been learned in other fields of knowledge. The existence of disciplines presumes clearly defined objects of analysis amenable to closed system analysis. Moreover, the critical capacities of members of a discipline are constrained by the limitations on what they can theorize and the methods they can employ.

- *Interdisciplinary knowledge* is credited with leading to the generation of interesting new questions, posing problems in new ways, and shaking up complacency. However, once the questions have been posed, this tends to produce a retreat back into disciplinary research in order to answer these new questions. Multidisciplinary research often attempts to draw together the work of different fields of knowledge but tends to bolt the work together in an unintegrated way. On the positive side, objects of analysis are seen as complex and multidimensional, but there is still a tendency to view objects as definite objective entities, neglecting the representational and symbolic aspects of knowledge production.
- *Postdisciplinary knowledge* assumes that it is possible to establish connections between the ways these questions are addressed across the social sciences and develop social research which regards the boundaries established by disciplinary and interdisciplinary social science as permeable. A postdisciplinary approach acknowledges objects of analysis as complex contested spaces. Moreover, the acceptance of methodological pluralism creates a context in which there are greater opportunities for innovation and critical reflexivity, taking account of the relations between readers and writers in social research.

Through disciplinary discourses and the emergence of organized academic communities (such as professional associations and the development of a compartmentalized departmental institutional structure) meaning production in academic work became intensely regulated. Yet the destabilization of disciplinary discourses means that objects of analysis are no longer seen as simple, certain and well defined (but, as suggested earlier, are now understood as complex, uncertain and contested spaces). What we may be witnessing is the gradual emergence of the first postdisciplinary academic discourses. As with disciplinary discourses, we should distinguish two interconnected dimensions.

- The *discursive dimension* of a postdisciplinary approach not only highlights capacity for self-reference and self-regulation (autopoiesis) but also acknowledges the ways within which meanings are produced by audiences as well as social scientists. They attempt to open up the possibility of alternative interpretations and recognize that their work is plausible within the terms of the stock of common-sense knowledge of different audiences. Textual sources will not be seen as unquestionable points of reference and the institutional practices through which we classify people will be conducted in a more sensitive way, so that it does not shore up the inclusionary and exclusionary relations of everyday life which lead to injustice. This will also be achieved through the construction of subject positions in which an investment of identity will not lead to disempowerment.

- The *knowledge dimension* of a postdisciplinary approach will acknowledge the system of language and specific cultural values, the rules of conduct and the established social practices, as well the institutional and textual conditions of knowledge production. In short, it must redefine objects of analysis inherited from disciplinary studies, drawing upon concepts, arguments and evidence in a way which avoids partial and one-sided accounts. Of particular importance is being aware of the way we draw upon and articulate classificatory systems in order to engage in social research practices. It is not only the way we locate people in categories that must be challenged. We should destabilize the classificatory systems responsible for pathologies; classification systems are negotiated and are not fixed inventories.

This book has considered a variety of approaches from cultural analysis many of which are usually associated with poststructuralism and phenomenology. Other approaches to knowledge construction exist. For example, the critical realist approach has also acknowledged the problems of closed systems in studying both natural and social objects. I have discussed this at length elsewhere (Smith 1998b: ch. 7; see also Smith 2000). Some exponents of critical realism have begun to develop a postdisciplinary account of the social and have been explicitly critical of the parochialism and imperialism of disciplinary projects (Sayer 1999). Broadly speaking, critical realism holds a contradictory position in discussing the normality/pathology distinction. On the one hand, in the transformational model of social action (Bhaskar 1979) it offers an account of how knowledge can emancipate the pathologized from unwanted determinations. Yet, the reluctance to address the symbolic and classificatory systems at work in social science is a major problem for this approach. I hope I can encourage many of the critical realist movement to take representation, culture and discourse much more seriously as a realm of study. More cogently for our concerns here, critical realism is often concerned to identify unobservable social relations and uses 'disorders', 'breakdowns' and 'dysfunctionality' in order to specify the normal. Certainly we need better accounts of the processes of normalization to match the growing work on pathologies, but I am not convinced that reproducing the language of disorder and abnormality in such a direct way is the best way to approach it. In addition, the textual approach in realism is often strictly readerly and tries to close down opportunities for its audiences, especially social researchers, to rewrite the arguments involved in ways which enable them to deal adequately with their chosen research.

By questioning 'canonicity' we can begin to unravel the mechanisms through which disciplinarity in the social sciences has been established. The debates that have featured around the concept of culture, its production, classification and consumption and the relationship between these and the production of meaning have provided contemporary social sciences with a once in a lifetime opportunity to break with the restraints that disciplinarity imposes. Examples of transdisciplinary approaches in the study of material cultures, social problems, conversational analysis and the discourses of the body, to name a few, provide some of the ways in which we could break with the scriptural economy. Of course, as indicated in the opening chapter, 'culture' is not the answer. There are especially strong parallels between cultural elitism and disciplinarity in social scientific practice. The problems created by converting culturally specific values into classificatory practices which remain tacit will not go away. We should not assume that the word 'culture' can act as a magic wand; it is what we do with it that counts.

References

Adorno, T. W. (1941) 'On popular music', *Studies in Philosophy and Social Sciences*, 9: 17–48.

Althusser, L. (1965) 'Contradiction and overdetermination' in *For Marx*. London: New Left Books.

Althusser, L. (1971) *Lenin and Philosophy and Other Essays*. London: New Left Books.

Althusser, L. and Balibar, E. (1968) *Reading Capital*. London: New Left Books.

Austin, J. (1962) *How To Do Things with Words*. London: Oxford University Press.

Bakhtin, M. (1981) *The Dialogic Imagination: Four Essays*. Austin, TX: Texas University Press.

Bakhtin, M. (1984) *Rabelais and his World*. Bloomington, IN: Indiana University Press.

Barthes, R. (1970) *S/Z*. London: Cape.

Barthes, R. (1973) *Mythologies*. London: Fontana.

Barthes, R. (1976) *The Pleasure of the Text*. London: Cape.

Barthes, R. (1977) *Image Music Text*. London: Fontana.

Beccaria, C. de (1764/1963) *Dei Delitti E Delle Pene (On Crime and Punishments)*. New York: Bobbs-Merrill.

Beirne, P. (1991) 'Inventing criminology: the "Science of Man" in Cesare Beccaria's *Dei Delitti E Delle Pene*', *Criminology*, 29(4): 777–820.

Bellah, R. (1976) 'New religious consciousness and the crisis of modernity' in R. Bellah and C. Y. Glock (eds), *The New Religious Consciousness*. Berkeley, CA: University of California Press.

Berger, A. A. (1998) *Media Analysis Techniques*, 2nd edition. London: Sage.

Bhaskar, R. (1979) *The Possibility of Naturalism: A Philosophical Critique of the Contemporary Human Sciences*. Brighton: Harvester Wheatsheaf.

Bhaskar, R. (1989) *The Possibility of Naturalism: A Philosophical Critique of the Contemporary Human Sciences*, 2nd edition. Hemel Hempstead: Harvester Wheatsheaf.

Blalock, H. (1964) *Causal Inferences in Non-Experimental Research.* Chapel Hill, NC: University of North Carolina Press.

Bourdieu, P. (1984) *Distinction: A Social Critique of the Judgement of Taste.* London: Routledge.

Brown, V. (1994) *Adam Smith's Discourses: Canonicity, Commerce and Conscience.* London: Routledge.

Burman, E., Aitken, G., Alldred, P. *et al.* (eds) (1996) *Psychology, Discourse and Social Practice: From Regulation to Resistance.* London: Taylor & Francis.

Burt, C. (1925/1961) *The Young Delinquent*, 4th edition. London: University of London Press.

Certeau, M. de (1984) *The Practice of Everyday Life.* Berkeley, CA: University of California Press.

Cicourel, A. (1976) *The Social Organisation of Juvenile Justice.* London: Heinemann.

Clarke, A. J. (1997) 'Tupperware: suburbia, sociology and mass consumption' in R. Silverstone (ed.) *Visions of Suburbia.* London: Routledge.

Clarke, J. (1975) 'The skinheads and the magical recovery of community' in S. Hall and T. Jefferson (eds) *Resistance through Rituals: Youth Subcultures in Post-war Britain.* London: HarperCollins.

Clarke, J. (1998) 'The trouble with normal', inaugural professorial lecture. Mimeo, The Open University.

Clarke, J. and Cochrane, A. (1998) 'The social construction of social problems' in E. Saraga (ed.) *Embodying the Social: Constructions of Difference.* London: Sage.

Cohen, S. (1972/1987) *Folk Devils and Moral Panics: The Creation of Mods and Rockers.* Oxford: Blackwell.

Cooley, C. H. (1902) *Human Nature and the Social Order.* New York: Schribner's.

Dahl, R. (1957) 'The concept of power', *Behavioral Science*, 2: 201–5.

Dahl, R. (1961) *Who Governs? Democracy and Power in an American City.* New Haven, CT: Yale University Press.

Derrida, J. (1973) *Speech and Phenomena.* Evanston, IL: Northwestern University Press.

Derrida, J. (1976) *Of Grammatology.* Baltimore, MD: Johns Hopkins University Press.

Derrida, J. (1978) *Writing and Difference.* London: Routledge.

Derrida, J. (1981) *Positions.* London: Athlone Press.

Donzelot, J. (1979) *The Policing of Families.* London: Hutchinson.

Douglas, M. (1966) *Purity and Danger: An Analysis of Pollution and Taboo.* London: Routledge.

Durkheim, E. ([1912]1976) *The Elementary Forms of Religious Life*. London: Allen and Unwin.

Durkheim, E. and Mauss, M. (1963) *Primitive Classification*. London: Cohen and West.

Easthope, A. and McGowan, K. (eds) (1992) *A Critical and Cultural Theory Reader*. Buckingham: Open University Press.

Eco, U. (1984) *Semiotics and the Philosophy of Language*. London: Macmillan.

Edwards, D. and Potter, J. (1993) *Discursive Psychology*. London: Sage.

Farquhar, D. (1996) *The Other Machine: Discourses and Reproductive Technologies*. London: Routledge.

Feeley, M. M. and Simon, J. (1992) 'The new penology: notes on the emerging strategy of corrections and its implications', *Criminology*, 30(4): 449–74.

Fernando, S., Ndegwa, D. and Wilson, M. (1997) *Forensic Psychiatry, Race and Culture*. London: Routledge.

Feyerabend, P. (1978) *Science for a Free Society*. London: New Left Books.

Fiddes, N. (1991) *Meat: A Natural Symbol*. London: Routledge.

Foucault, M. (1967) *Madness and Civilisation: A History of Insanity in the Age of Reason*. London; Tavistock/Routledge.

Foucault, M. (1970) *The Order of Things*. London: Tavistock.

Foucault, M. (1972) *The Archaeology of Knowledge*. London: Tavistock.

Foucault, M. (1973) *The Birth of the Clinic: An Archaeology of Medical Perception*. London: Tavistock/Routledge.

Foucault, M. (1977) *Discipline and Punish*. Harmondsworth: Penguin.

Foucault, M. (1980) *Power/Knowledge: Selected Interviews and Other Writings 1972–1977*. Brighton: Harvester Press.

Foucault, M. (1982) 'The subject and power' in H. L. Dreyfus and P. Rabinow (eds), *Michel Foucault: Beyond Structuralism and Hermeneutics*. Brighton: Harvester Press.

Garfinkel, H. (1967) *Studies in Ethnomethodology*. Englewood Cliffs, NJ: Prentice-Hall.

Gendron, B. (1986) 'Theodor Adorno meets the Cadillacs' in T. Modleski (ed.), *Studies in Entertainment: Critical Approaches to Mass Culture*. Bloomington, IN: Indiana University Press.

Giddens, A. (1982a) *Profiles and Critiques in Social Theory*. Basingstoke: Macmillan.

Giddens, A. (1982b) 'Power, the dialectic of control and class structuration' in A. Giddens and G. Mackenzie (eds) *Social Class and the Division of Labour*. Cambridge: Cambridge University Press.

Gilroy, P. (1993) *The Black Atlantic: Modernity and Double Consciousness*. London: Verso.

Gramsci, A. (1971) *Selections from Prison Notebooks*. London: Lawrence and Wishart.

Guillaumin, C. (1995) *Racism, Sexism, Power and Ideology.* London: Routledge.

Hall, S. (1973) 'Encoding and decoding in television discourses', Centre for Contemporary Cultural Studies (CCCS) Stencilled Paper 7, Birmingham: CCCS; published in an abridged version as 'Encoding/decoding' in S. Hall, D. Hobson, A. Lowe and P. Willis (eds), *Culture, Media, Language.* London: Hutchinson.

Hall, S. (1980) 'Popular-democratic vs. Authoritarian Populism: two ways of taking democracy seriously' in A. Hunt (ed.), *Marxism and Democracy.* London: Lawrence and Wishart.

Hall, S. (1981) 'Notes on deconstructing the popular' in R. Samuel (ed.), *People's History and Socialist Theory.* London: Routledge.

Hall, S. (1983a) 'The great moving right show' in S. Hall and M. Jacques (eds) *The Politics of Thatcherism.* London: Lawrence and Wishart.

Hall, S. (1983b) 'The little Caesars of social democracy' in S. Hall and M. Jacques (eds) *The Politics of Thatcherism.* London: Lawrence and Wishart.

Hall, S. (1992) 'The West and the Rest: discourse and power' in S. Hall and B. Gieben (eds), *Formations of Modernity.* Cambridge: Polity.

Hall, S. (1997) 'The work of representation' in S. Hall (ed.), *Representation: Cultural Representations and Signifying Practices.* London: Sage.

Hall, S. and Jefferson, T. (eds) (1975) *Resistance through Rituals: Youth Subcultures in Post-war Britain.* London: HarperCollins.

Hall, S. and Whannel, P. (1964) *The Popular Arts.* London: Hutchinson.

Hall, S., Critcher, C., Jefferson, T., Clarke, J. and Roberts, B. (1978) *Policing the Crisis: Mugging, the State, and Law and Order.* London: Macmillan.

Haraway, D. (1991) *Simians, Cyborgs, and Women: The Reinvention of Nature.* London: Routledge.

Harding, S. (1986) *The Science Question in Feminism.* Milton Keynes: Open University Press.

Harré, R. (1979) *Social Being.* Oxford: Blackwell.

Harré, R. (1991) *Physical Being: A Theory for Corporeal Psychology.* Oxford: Blackwell.

Harré, R. and Gillett, G. (1994) *The Discursive Mind.* London: Sage.

Harré, R. and Krausz, M. (1996) *Varieties of Relativism.* Oxford: Blackwell.

Harré, R. and Secord, P. F. (1973) *The Explanation of Social Behaviour.* Oxford: Blackwell.

Hawkes, T. (1977) *Structuralism and Semiotics.* London: Methuen.

Hebdige, D. (1975) 'The meaning of Mod' in S. Hall and T. Jefferson (eds), *Resistance through Rituals: Youth Subcultures in Post-war Britain.* London: HarperCollins.

Hebdige, D. (1979) *Subculture: The Meaning of Style.* London: Methuen.

Hewitt, D. and Owusu-Bempah, J. (1994) *The Racism of Psychology: Time for Change.* Englewood Cliffs, NJ: Prentice-Hall.

Hoggart, R. (1957) *The Uses of Literacy*. Harmondsworth: Penguin.

Hoggart, R. (1995) *The Way We Live Now*. London: Chatto and Windus.

Hinchcliffe, S. (1999) 'Cities and natures: intimate strangers' in J. Allen, D. Massey and M. Pryke (eds), *Unsettling Cities: Movement/Settlement*. London: Routledge.

Horkheimer, M. and Adorno, T. (1947/1979) *Dialectic of Enlightenment*. London: Verso.

Humphreys, L. (1970) *Tearoom Trade: Impersonal Sex in Public Places*. Chicago: Aldine.

Humphries, S. and Gordon, P. (1993) *A Labour of Love: The Experience of Parenthood in Britain 1900–1950*. London: Sidgwick and Jackson.

Illich, I. (1971) *Deschooling Society*. London: Calder and Boyers.

Jefferson, T. (1975) 'Cultural responses of the Teds: the defence of space and status' in S. Hall and T. Jefferson (eds), *Resistance through Rituals: Youth Subcultures in Post-war Britain*. London: HarperCollins.

Jeffery, R. (1979) 'Normal rubbish: deviant patients in a casualty department' in D. Kelly (ed.) *Deviant Behavior*, 3rd edn. New York: St Martin's Press.

Jenkins, H. (1992) *Textual Poachers*. London: Routledge.

Kant, I. (1790/1987) *Critique of Judgement*. Indianapolis, IN: Hackett.

Keat, R. and Urry, J. (1978) *Social Theory as Science*, 2nd edition. London: Routledge.

Laclau, E. (1977) *Politics and Ideology in Marxist Theory*. London: Verso.

Laclau, E. (1990) *New Reflections on the Revolution of our Time*. London: Verso.

Laclau, E. and Mouffe, C. (1985) *Hegemony and Socialist Strategy: Towards a Radical Democratic Politics*. London: Verso.

Lakatos, I. (1970) 'Falsification and the methodology of scientific research programmes' in I. Lakatos and A. Musgrave (eds), *Criticism and the Growth of Knowledge*. Cambridge: Cambridge University Press.

Latour, B. and Woolgar, S. (1979) *Laboratory Life: The Construction of Scientific Facts*. Princeton, NJ: Princeton University Press.

Leavis, F. R. (1930) *Mass Civilisation and Minority Culture*. Cambridge: Minority Press.

Leavis, F. R. and Thompson, D. (1933) *Culture and Environment: The Training of Critical Awareness*. London: Chatto and Windus.

Leopold, A. (1949) *A Sand County Almanac – and Sketches Here and There*. Oxford: Oxford University Press.

Lévi-Strauss, C. (1949/1969) *The Elementary Structures of Kinship*. London: Eyre and Spottiswoode.

Lévi-Strauss, C. (1963) *Structural Anthropology*. New York: Basic Books.

Lidchi, H. (1997) 'The poetics and the politics of exhibiting other cultures' in S. Hall (ed.), *Representation: Cultural Representations and Signifying Practices*. London: Sage.

Littlewood, R. and Lipsedge, M. (1997) *Aliens and Alienists: Ethnic Minorities and Psychiatry*, 3rd edition. London: Routledge.

Lombroso, C. (1876/1911) *L'Uomo delinquente (The Criminal Man)*. London: Penguin.

Lombroso, C. and Ferrero, W. (1895/1915) *The Female Offender*. New York: D. Appleton.

Lukács, G. (1923/1971) *History and Class Consciousness*. London: Merlin.

Lukács, G. (1957/1963) *The Meaning of Contemporary Realism*. London: Merlin.

Lyon, D. (1994) *Postmodernity*. Buckingham: Open University Press.

McCloskey, D. (1983) 'The rhetoric of economics', *Journal of Economic Literature*, 21: 481–571.

McNay, L. (1992) *Foucault and Feminism: Power, Gender and the Self*. Cambridge: Polity.

McNay, L. (1994) *Foucault: A Critical Introduction*. Cambridge: Polity.

McRobbie, A. and Garber, J. (1975) 'Girls and subcultures' in S. Hall and T. Jefferson (eds) *Resistance through Rituals: Youth Subcultures in Post-war Britain*. London: HarperCollins.

Mauss, M. (1990) *The Gift*. London: Routledge.

Marcuse, H. (1972) *One Dimensional Man*. London: Abacus.

Markham, A. (1994) *A Brief History of Pollution*. London: Earthscan.

Massey, D. (1994) *Space, Place and Gender*. Cambridge: Polity.

Massey, D. (1995) 'The conceptualisation of space' in D. Massey and P. Jess (eds), *A Place in the World*. Oxford: Oxford University Press.

Massey, D. (1999) 'On space and the city' in D. Massey, J. Allen and S. Pile (eds), *City Worlds*. London: Routledge.

Mead, G. H. (1934) *Mind, Self and Society*, ed. C. W. Morris. Chicago: University of Chicago Press.

Meens, R. (1995) 'Pollution in the early middle ages: the case of the food regulations in the penitentials', *Early Medieval Europe*, 4(1): 3–19.

Midgley, M. (1996) *Utopias, Dolphins and Computers: Problems in Philosophical Plumbing*. London: Routledge.

Miller, D. (ed.) (1995) *Acknowledging Comsumption: A Review of New Studies*. London: Routledge.

Miller, D. (1997) 'Consumption and its consequences' in H. Mackay (ed.), *Consumption and Everyday Life*. London: Sage.

Miller, D. (ed.) (1998) *Material Cultures: Why Some Things Matter*. London: UCL Press.

Morley, D. (1980) *The Nationwide Audience*. London: British Film Institute.

Morley, D. (1995) 'Theories of consumption in media studies' in D. Miller (ed.), *Acknowledging Comsumption: A Review of New Studies*. London: Routledge.

Morley, D. and Silverstone, R. (1990) 'Domestic communications: technologies and meanings', *Media, Culture and Society*, 12(1): 31–55.

Muir, J. (1901) *Our National Parks*. Boston, MA: Houghton Mifflin.

Mulkay, M. (1991) *Sociology of Science: A Sociological Pilgrimage*. Buckingham: Open University Press.

Newman, G. and Marongiu, P. (1990) 'Penological reform and the myth of Beccaria', *Criminology*, 28(2): 325–46.

Parker, H. (1974) *View from the Boys*. Newton Abbot: David and Charles.

Parker, I. (1992) *Discourse Dynamics: Critical Analysis for Social and Individual Psychology*. London: Routledge.

Parker, I. (ed.) (1999) *Critical Textwork*. Buckingham: Open University Press.

Parker, I., Goergaca, E., Harper, D. and McLaughlin, T. (1995) *Deconstructing Psychopathology*. London: Sage.

Patrick, J. (1973) *A Glasgow Gang Observed*. London: Eyre-Methuen.

Pile, S. and Thrift, N. (eds) (1995) *Mapping the Subject: Geographies of Cultural Transformation*. London: Routledge.

Pinchot, G. (1901) *The Fight for Conservation*. New York: Harcourt Brace.

Popper, K. (1959) *The Logic of Scientific Discovery*. London: Hutchinson.

Popper, K. (1963) *Conjectures and Refutations: The Growth of Scientific Knowledge*. London: Routledge.

Porter, R. (1987) *A Social History of Madness*. London: Weidenfeld and Nicolson.

Potter, J. and Wetherell, M. (1987) *Discourse and Social Psychology: Beyond Attitudes and Behaviour*. London: Sage.

Poulantzas, N. (1978) *State, Power, Socialism*. London: New Left Books.

Propp, V. (1928/1958) *Morphology of the Folktale*. Austin, TX: University of Texas Press.

Propp, V. (1984) *Theory and History of Folklore*. Manchester: Manchester University Press.

Richards, G. (1997) *'Race', Racism and Psychology: Towards a Reflexive History*. London: Routledge.

Rorty, R. (1994) 'Method, social science and social hope' in S. Seidman (ed.), *The Postmodern Turn: New Perspectives in Social Theory*. Cambridge: Cambridge University Press.

Said, E. (1978) *Orientalism*. London: Routledge.

Saussure, F. de (1916/1959) *Course in General Linguistics*. London: Collins.

Sayer, A. (1999) 'Long live postdisciplinary studies!', paper for the British Sociology Association Conference, April, Glasgow, mimeo.

Schütz, A. (1932/1967) *The Phenomenology of the Social World*. Evanston, IL: North Western University Press.

Schütz, A. (1943) 'The problem of rationality in the social world', *Economica*, 10 (May): 130–49.

Schütz, A. (1953) 'Common-sense and scientific interpretation of human action', *Philosophy and Phenomenological Research*, 14(1): 1–38.

Shaw, C. R. (1930) *The Jack Roller: A Delinquent Boy's Own Story*. Chicago: University of Chicago Press.

Sheldon, W. H. (1949) *Varieties of Delinquent Youth*. New York: Harper and Brothers.

Smith, A. M. (1994) *New Right Discourses on Race and Sexuality: Britain 1968–1990.* Cambridge: Cambridge University Press.

Smith, M. J. (1998a) *Ecologism: Towards Ecological Citizenship.* Buckingham: Open University Press and Minneapolis, MN: University of Minnesota Press.

Smith, M. J. (1998b) *Social Science in Question: Towards a Postdisciplinary Framework.* London: Sage.

Smith, M. J. (ed.) (1999) *Thinking through the Environment.* London: Routledge.

Smith, M. J. (2000) *Rethinking State Theory,* Routledge Innovations in Political Theory 3. London: Routledge.

Sontag, S. (1989) *AIDS and its Metaphors.* New York: Farrar, Strauss and Giroux.

Sparks, C. (1996) 'Stuart Hall, cultural studies and Marxism' in D. Morley and K. H. Chen (eds), *Stuart Hall: Critical Dialogues in Cultural Studies.* London: Routledge.

Sparks, R. (1996) 'Prisons, punishment and penalty' in E. McLaughlin and J. Muncie (eds), *Controlling Crime.* London: Sage.

Thompson, E. P. (1961a) 'The long revolution', *New Left Review,* 9(May–June): 24–33.

Thompson, E. P. (1961b) 'The long revolution II', *New Left Review,* 10(July–August): 34–9.

Thompson, E. P. (1963) *The Making of the English Working Class.* Harmondsworth: Penguin.

Thornton, S. (1995) *Club Cultures: Music, Media and Subcultural Capital.* Cambridge: Polity.

Tuan, Y. F. (1974) *Topophilia.* Englewood Cliffs, NJ: Prentice-Hall.

Tuan, Y. F. (1978) 'The city – its distance from nature', *Geographical Review,* 68(1): 1–12.

Tuan, Y. F. (1984) *Dominance and Affection: The Making of Pets.* New Haven, CT: Yale University Press.

Turner, B. (1995) *Medical Power and Social Knowledge,* 2nd edition. London: Sage.

Voloshinov, V. N. (1929/1973) *Marxism and the Philosophy of Language.* New York: Seminar Press.

Weeks, J. (1985) *Sexuality and its Discontents.* London: Routledge.

Weeks, J. (1989) *Sex, Politics and Society: The Regulation of Sexuality since 1800,* 2nd edition. London: Longman.

Williams, R. (1958) *Culture and Society 1780–1950.* Harmondsworth: Penguin.

Williams, R. (1961) *The Long Revolution.* London: Chatto and Windus.

Williams, R. (1983) *Keywords: A Vocabulary of Culture and Society,* 2nd edition. London: Fontana.

Willis, P. (1977) *Learning to Labour: How Working Class Kids Get Working Class Jobs.* Farnborough: Saxon House.

Willis, P. (1990) *Common Culture: Symbolic Work at Play in the Everyday Cultures of the Young*. Buckingham: Open University Press.

Wright, W. (1975) *Sixguns and Society: A Structural Study of the Western*. Berkeley, CA: University of California Press.

Index

MATERIAL CULTURE IN THE SOCIAL WORLD

Tim Dant

This should become a core text for second year courses in
sociology and cultural studies . . . it synthesizes a vast body of
literature and a complex range of debates into a text which is
at once accessible, engaging and stimulating . . . it will lead to
students seeing and thinking about the material world in a
totally new light and can be used as a way into key theoretical
debates.

Keith Tester, Professor of Social Theory, University of
Portsmouth

- In what ways do we interact with material things?
- How do material objects affect the way we relate to each other?
- What are the connections between material things and social pro-
cesses like fashion, discourse, art and design?

Through wearing clothes, keeping furniture, responding to the ring
of the telephone, noticing the signature on a painting, holding a
paperweight and in many other ways, we interact with objects in our
everyday lives. These are not merely functional relationships with
things but are connected to the way we relate to other people and
the culture of the particular society we live in – they are social
relations. This engaging book draws on established theoretical
work, including that of Simmel, Marx, McLuhan, Barthes and Bau-
drillard as well as a range of contemporary empirical work from
many humanities disciplines. It uses ideas drawn from this work to
explore a variety of things – from stone cairns to denim jeans, tele-
visions to penis rings, houses to works of art – to understand something of how we live with them.

Contents

*Introduction: the cairn and the mini-strip – Consuming or living with
things? – Fetishism and the social value of objects – Building and
dwelling – Wearing it out: written and material clothing – Playing with
things: interacting with a windsurfer – Objects in time: modernity and
biography – Turn it on: objects that mediate – Who's that? People as
objects – Conclusion – Further reading – Bibliography – Index.*

240pp   0 335 19821 X (Paperback)   0 335 19822 8 (Hardback)

CINEMA AND CULTURAL MODERNITY

Gill Branston

- What is the relationship of popular cinema to the concept of 'modernity'?
- What now are the key areas of debate which focus the study of cinema and its audiences?
- How can we understand the relationship of cinema to both the pleasures of consumerism and the inequalities addressed by critical politics?

Cinema and Cultural Modernity carves a lucid path through the central debates of film and cinema studies and explores these in their social and political contexts. The book includes histories of the ways in which we view Hollywood's global dominance, up to the development of late modernity and the declaration of 'postmodernity'. In an accessible fashion, it discusses changing theorizations of the economics, audiences, and fascinations of cinema, addressing concepts such as agency, negotiation and identification, and global 'popularity' within contemporary cultures of celebrity, consumption and the visual. Gill Branston outlines the need for cinema study that is both sensitive to the formal 'textiness' of films, but also less anxious about arguing for its position within broad agendas of representation. At the same time, the author links such areas to both the pleasures of consumption, which cinema so often evokes and embodies, and to the need for a new, critical politics to address the persistent inequalities of modernity, inequalities which still fuel lively interest in questions of representation. The result is an inclusive text for undergraduate courses and an essential reference for researchers.

Contents

Introduction – Hollywood histories – 'New again' Hollywood – 'Globally popular' cinema? – Authors and agency – Stars, bodies, galaxies – Movies move audiences – Identifying a critical politics of representation – Glossary – Bibliography – Index.

224pp   0 335 20076 1 (Paperback)   0 335 20077 X (Hardback)

MULTICULTURALISM

C. W. Watson

- Is multiculturalism compatible with national identity?
- Does multiculturalism simply mean a tolerance of cultural diversity?
- Does globalization spell the end of multiculturalism?

Multicultural and multiculturalism are words frequently used to describe the ethnic diversity that exists everywhere in the world today. However, there is some confusion about what precisely they signify. Do they simply describe diversity or are they advocating a particular response to that diversity? This book looks at some of the debates associated with these words and with the concepts attached to them. In particular the arguments for and against multiculturalism are examined in the context of modern states in different political and historical circumstances. Attitudes and emphases in relation to multiculturalism differ, it is argued, from one country to another and the chapters of the book draw out the dimensions of difference with examples ranging from Europe and the USA to South-East Asia and China. The focus of the discussion is placed on issues such as minority rights, education, religious tolerance and the trend to global homogenization. The result is a concise and balanced overview of a topic with wide appeal across undergraduate and postgraduate courses from sociology and politics to cultural studies and anthropology.

Contents
Introduction – Nationalism and multiculturalism – Education, religion and the media – Cultural diversity and global uniformity – Multiculturalism in historical perspective – Conclusion – References – Index.

136pp   0 335 20520 8 (Paperback)   0 335 20521 6 (Hardback)

Index

Credits